Test Yourself

English Grammar

Elaine Bender, M.A.
El Camino College, Torrance, CA
Pasadena City College, Pasadena, CA

Contributing Editors

Bruce Kirle, M.A.
Trident Technical College
Charleston, SC

Colleen Lloyd, M.A.
Cuyahoga Community College
Cleveland, OH

E. Carole McClanahan, M.Ed.
Danville Community College
Danville, VA

NTC LEARNINGWORKS
a division of NTC Publishing Group
Lincolnwood, Illinois

Library of Congress Cataloging-in-Publication Data
is available from the Library of Congress.

A *Test Yourself Books, Inc.* Project

Published by NTC Publishing Group
© 1996 NTC Publishing Group, 4255 West Touhy Avenue
Lincolnwood (Chicago), Illinois 60646-1975 U.S.A.

6 7 8 9 ML 0 9 8 7 6 5 4 3 2 1

Contents

Preface

Writing is a public act. For writing to communicate to the reader, both the writer and the reader must know the rules of the written language. It is the writer's obligation to follow the rules so that the reader can understand what the writer is expressing. Grammar is the study of the rules that control written (and spoken) language.

Grammar resembles law. Like law, grammar is made up of a body of rules that are related to one another. To understand the rules, one must know the definitions of the terms used in the rules. Then one must be able to apply the general rules to a specific situation. In law, one applies the rules to the facts of a case. In grammar, the rules are applied to the words, phrases, clauses, and sentences of discourse. Just as different jurisdictions have different laws, every language has its own grammar. This book tests your knowledge of the rules of the grammar of American English. It is not a grammar text or review book. It assumes you already know the definitions of basic terms in grammar and that you are familiar with the most common grammar rules.

Each section in a chapter begins with a description of the subtopics covered in that section. Examples and explanations are also provided. After you read the introductory material at the beginning of each section, take the tests that follow that information. Then check your answers against those given at the end of the chapter. The correct responses are given, with explanations. If you have more than three incorrect responses for a ten-question test, you need to review the subtopic for that test. If the test is longer, review if you have more than three incorrect answers for each multiple of ten questions.

Several people made it possible for me to write this book. I thank my father, Louis Feinberg, who taught me about law and logic by example and precept. Professor David Ohara of Alfred University taught me about discipline in writing. Mel Homer's patience, psychological acuity, and affection have been an inspiration and support to me.

This book is dedicated to the memory of my mother, Sylvia Epstein Feinberg.

Elaine Bender

How to Use this Book

This "Test Yourself" book is part of a unique series designed to help you improve your test scores on almost any type of examination you will face. Too often, you will study for a test—quiz, midterm, or final—and come away with a score that is lower than anticipated. Why? Because there is no way for you to really know how much you understand a topic until you've taken a test. The *purpose* of the test, after all, is to test your complete understanding of the material.

The "Test Yourself" series offers you a way to improve your scores and to actually test your knowledge at the time you use this book. Consider each chapter a diagnostic pretest in a specific topic. Answer the questions, check your answers, and then give yourself a grade. Then, and only then, will you know where your strengths and, more importantly, weaknesses are. Once these areas are identified, you can strategically focus your study on those topics that need additional work.

Each book in this series presents a specific subject in an organized manner, and although each "Test Yourself" chapter may not correspond to exactly the same chapter in your textbook, you should have little difficulty in locating the specific topic you are studying. Written by educators in the field, each book is designed to correspond, as much as possible, to the leading textbooks. This means that you can feel confident in using this book, and that regardless of your textbook, professor, or school, you will be much better prepared for anything you will encounter on your test.

Each chapter has four parts:

Brief Yourself. All chapters contain a brief overview of the topic that is intended to give you a more thorough understanding of the material with which you need to be familiar. Sometimes this information is presented at the beginning of the chapter, and sometimes it flows throughout the chapter, to review your understanding of various *units* within the chapter.

Test Yourself. Each chapter covers a specific topic corresponding to one that you will find in your textbook. Answer the questions, either on a separate page or directly in the book, if there is room.

Check Yourself. Check your answers. Every question is fully answered and explained. These answers will be the key to your increased understanding. If you answered the question incorrectly, read the explanations to *learn* and *understand* the material. You will note that at the end of every answer you will be referred to a specific subtopic within that chapter, so you can focus your studying and prepare more efficiently.

Grade Yourself. At the end of each chapter is a self-diagnostic key. By indicating on this form the numbers of those questions you answered incorrectly, you will have a clear picture of your weak areas.

There are no secrets to test success. Only good preparation can guarantee higher grades. By utilizing this "Test Yourself" book, you will have a better chance of improving your scores and understanding the subject more fully.

Sentence Basics

1

Test Yourself

1.1 Types of Sentences Classified by Purpose

A *declarative sentence* makes a statement.

Example:

A column of ants crawled across the kitchen floor.

An *interrogative sentence* asks a question.

Example:

What do ants eat?

An *imperative sentence* expresses a command, instruction, or requests.

Example:

Clean up that mess!

An *exclamatory sentence* states a strong emotion.

Example:

I hate creepy crawling creatures!

Identify each sentence as D (declarative), IN (interrogative), IM (imperative), or E (exclamatory).

1. Look before you leap.

2. What is the meaning of this familiar proverb?

3. People should not jump to conclusions.

4. Do not undertake an action before considering its consequences.

5. Watch out!

6. I know I can ski-jump although I've never tried it.

7. What happened when you tried a ski jump for the first time?

8. It was a disaster!

9. He took the leap before he looked.

10. Take lessons before attempting a new sport.

1.2 Subjects and Predicates

The *subject* of a sentence names the person, thing, or quality the sentence is about. A simple subject consists of one word. In the sentence "Harry does card tricks," *Harry* is the simple subject. A compound subject names two or more persons, places, things, or qualities. In the sentence "Harry and Helen do magic tricks," *Harry and Helen* is the compound subject. The complete subject is the simple or compound subject and all the words that modify it. In the sentence "Harry and Helen, natives of Homestead, Virginia, performed magic tricks at the state fair," *Harry and Helen, natives of Homestead, Virginia* is the complete subject.

Prepositional phrases are never subjects by themselves; they may be part of the complete subject. In the sentence "A book of explanations of Houdini's magic tricks was published last month," *book* is the subject. *Of explanations of Houdini's magic tricks* combines two prepositional phrases. Neither one is the subject of the verb *was published*.

The *predicate* of a sentence tells what the subject does or is. A simple predicate has one verb. In the sentence "Harry does card tricks," *does card tricks* is the simple predicate. A compound predicate has two or more verbs describing the same subject. In the sentence "Harry does card tricks and escapes from locked trunks," *does card tricks and escapes from locked trunks* is the compound predicate. The complete predicate includes the verb and all the words that modify it. In the sentence "Harry does card tricks skillfully and escapes from locked trunks with ease," the complete predicate is *does card tricks skillfully and escapes from locked trunks with ease*.

For each of the sentences below, indicate if the subject is simple or compound, and if the predicate is simple or compound.

11. One of the greatest magicians of all time was Houdini.

12. After his birth in Budapest in 1874, he and his family moved to New York.

13. From the age of fourteen, he practiced and perfected magic tricks.

14. He, at the age of seventeen, became a professional magician.

15. For all of his professional life, he was famous for escape tricks.

16. Escaping from ropes and freeing himself from handcuffs amazed audiences.

17. One of his tricks was called the Metamorphosis Trick.

18. In this trick, with his hands bound, he escaped from a locked trunk.

19. On one occasion, four thousand people watched and applauded his daring handcuffed jump off a Pittsburgh bridge.

20. He, while underwater, freed himself in three minutes.

1.3 Clauses

A *clause* is a group of words containing a subject and a predicate.

Example:

Stephen Jay Gould writes essays.

An *independent clause* could stand alone as a complete sentence.

Example:

Stephen Jay Gould writes essays.

Although a *dependent clause* has a subject and verb, it cannot stand alone as a complete sentence.

Example:

After Stephen Jay Gould writes an essay.
Stephen Jay Gould, who writes essays.

Identify the underlined clause as independent (I) or dependent (D).

21. <u>When he was forty-two years old</u>, Stephen Jay Gould learned he was suffering from abdominal mesothelioma.

22. This is a serious cancer <u>that is usually associated with exposure to asbestos.</u>

23. Because he is a scientist, <u>he wanted to learn as much as he could about his condition</u>.

24. <u>He asked his doctor where to find technical literature about his disease</u> when he recovered after surgery.

25. <u>The doctor</u>, who knew what Gould would find, <u>did not want to help him.</u>

26. <u>After he studied the aspects of his disease,</u> Gould realized his situation.

27. <u>Whatever treatments were used</u>, mesothelioma was considered incurable.

28. Although the situation seemed hopeless, <u>Gould has survived</u>.

29. Gould is an evolutionary theorist <u>who teaches at Harvard University</u>.

30. While fulfilling his duties at Harvard, <u>he also writes popular scientific essays</u>.

1.4 Types of Sentences Classified by Clause Structure

A *simple sentence* consists of one independent *clause.*

Example:

Many hurricanes occurred in the Atlantic Ocean in 1995.

A *compound sentence* consists of two or more inde-*pendent clauses.*

Example:

Several hurricanes struck Florida; one storm devastated the Virgin Islands.

A *complex sentence* consists of one independent clause and one or more dependent clauses.

Example:

When this phenomenon was noticed, [dependent clause] scientists wondered what had caused it. [independent clause]

A *compound-complex sentence* consists of two or more independent clauses and one or more dependent clauses.

Example:

Changes in climate could explain the phenomenon; [independent clause] although scientists cannot be certain, [dependent clause] they think global warming may be part of the cause. [independent clause]

Identify each sentence as S (simple), CD (compound), CX (complex), or CC (compound-complex).

31. In 1992, Hurricane Andrew devastated southern Florida.

32. The Northridge earthquake, which struck Southern California on January 17, 1994, caused freeways to buckle.

33. Tornadoes are common in the Midwest and Southwest, and hurricanes often occur along the East Coast.

34. When tornado warnings sound, people seek shelter, yet they fear for their lives and property.

35. Natural disasters cannot be avoided, but being prepared can help one survive them.

36. Many California residents keep an earthquake kit.

37. The kits provide survival materials to use when an earthquake strikes.

38. They contain first-aid supplies, food, water, and tools.

39. The kits are meant to make a family self-sufficient for a few days, but in the event of a great quake, the supplies might be inadequate.

40. Whenever disasters occur, the Red Cross tries to help by setting up shelters for victims.

41. Kate Chopin's novel *The Awakening* and her short story "The Storm" are set in Louisiana; while both describe regional culture, their characters belong to different social classes.

42. It may seem odd to think of *The Wizard of Oz* as a disaster film, but the story is precipitated by a tornado.

43. When Hollywood makes disaster movies, the films often deal with problems caused by flawed technology.

44. *The Poseidon Adventure* and *The Towering Inferno* are two examples of this genre.

45. *The Andromeda Strain* could be called a disaster film; it is also a science-fiction movie.

46. Because the Ebola virus has no cure, an outbreak of the disease in Africa in 1995 frightened many people.

47. In 1665, an epidemic of bubonic plague in England killed many people.

48. When a great fire destroyed much of London in 1666, it killed many rats and fleas that were carriers of the plague.

49. In the fourteenth century in Europe, bubonic plague was widespread, and it was called the Black Death.

50. In the Old Testament, ten plagues were sent against Egypt to force the pharaoh to permit the Israelites to leave the country.

1.5 Correcting Fused Sentences and Comma Splices

When two independent clauses are joined by a comma, this is an error known as a *comma splice*.

Example:

E. B. White wrote several books for children, *Charlotte's Web* still attracts many readers.

When two independent clauses are joined without correct punctuation, this is an error known as a *fused sentence*, or a run-on sentence.

Example.

E. B. White wrote several books for children *Charlotte's Web* still attracts many readers.

Two independent clauses may be joined by a comma followed by a coordinating conjunction.

Example:

E. B. White wrote several books for children, and he was also a writer of essays and poetry.

Two independent clauses may be joined by a semi-colon.

Example:

E. B. White wrote several books for children; he was also a writer of essays and poetry.

Two independent clauses may be joined by a semi-colon followed by a conjunctive adverb. The conjunctive adverb may or may not be followed by a comma.

Example:

E. B. White wrote several books for children; however, he is better known for his essays.

If the following sentences are correct, mark them C. If the independent clauses are joined incorrectly, correct the sentence by adding or changing punctuation and adding words if necessary.

51. E. B. White's essay "Once More to the Lake" is a classic and many generations of readers have enjoyed it.

52. White writes about his childhood trips to the lake, and he compares them with taking his own son to the lake.

53. White notes changes in the vacation experience however he finds its essence is unchanged.

54. White describes the arrival, his room, and the other vacationers, but his focus is on the feelings these details evoke.

55. Concrete and specific details fill the essay its theme is an abstraction, the sense of mortality.

56. Some families enjoy vacationing at a lake others prefer to go to an ocean beach.

57. Carol's family vacations by camping or they may hike in a national park.

58. On her vacation, Natasha went to Santa Fe, New Mexico consequently she was able to attend both the Santa Fe Opera and the Santa Fe Chamber Music Festival.

59. Native Americans live in the pueblo in Taos, New Mexico they worship in the pueblo's ancient church.

60. The Amish of Pennsylvania retain their old traditions; therefore, they do not drive cars.

61. Disney provides Americans with two vacation spots, Disneyland is in Anaheim, California, and Disney World is in Orlando, Florida.

62. Some people think New York City is a nice place to visit but they would not want to live there.

63. New Yorkers suffer many inconveniences however many feel that the city's rewards make the effort of daily living worthwhile.

64. Joan Didion's writing portrays the essence of cities she has written about Las Vegas, Miami, Los Angeles, and New York.

65. Her essay "Marrying Absurd" is about Las Vegas; in it she describes the city's wedding chapels.

66. The National Aeronautics and Space Museum is extremely popular, it is part of the Smithsonian Institution.

67. Denver's altitude is high consequently, the baseballs hit at Coors Park travel farther than they would if hit at a sea-level ballpark like County Stadium in Milwaukee.

68. Chicago's two baseball teams, the White Sox and Cubs, are in different leagues, and residents of the city are fans of one team or the other.

69. Similarly, in New York, Yankee fans don't root for the Mets and Mets fans don't go to Yankee Stadium.

70. In 1995, Hideo Nomo became a pitcher for the Los Angeles Dodgers, he is the first Japanese person to play on an American major league team.

1.6 Correcting Sentence Fragments

A group of words with a verb but no subject is a *sentence fragment*.

Example:

Reads about hobbies.

A group of words with a subject but no verb is a *sentence fragment*. Infinitives and verb forms ending in -ing are not verbs.

Examples:

Milly to read about furniture repair. Ricardo reading about historical monuments.

Some sentence fragments lack both a subject and a verb.

Example:

Interesting information about antiques.

A dependent clause standing alone is a *sentence fragment*.

Example:

Although the book discusses antiques.

Some of the following statements are complete sentences. Some are sentence fragments. Rewrite the statements to form a paragraph with no sentence fragments. You may add words, connect statements, and change punctuation as necessary. Items 71 through 80 form one paragraph. Items 81 through 90 form a second paragraph.

71. Anne's hobby is restoring old furniture.

72. Useful items like chairs, tables, and desks.

73. To earn extra money.

74. A leg on a kitchen chair was loose.

75. Using some new wood, she made a replacement leg.

76. After sanding the leg.

77. Carefully and neatly varnishing the leg.

78. Finished the job.

79. Because the chair was safer as well as more attractive.

80. Whoever bought the chair.

81. The Statue of Liberty was dedicated in New York in 1886.

82. A gift from the French people.

83. Who contributed funds for its construction in Paris.

84. Commemorating the friendship of the people of France and the people of the United States.

85. It was made of hundreds of copper sheets.

86. Hammered into shape by hand.

87. After it was finished.

88. It was disassembled and shipped to New York.

89. The Statue holds a torch in her right hand.

90. On her head a crown with seven spokes.

1.7 Identifying Sentence Patterns

There are five basic sentence patterns in English.

1. *Subject-verb*

Example:

Students write.

2. *Subject-verb-direct object*

Example:

Students write research papers.

3. *Subject-verb-direct object-object complement*

Example:

The Writers Club elected Jake Barney president for this term.

4. *Subject-verb-indirect object-direct object*

Example:

A student wrote the newspaper editor a letter.

5. *Subject-linking verb-subject complement.*

Examples:

The assignment is a research paper. The assignment is difficult.

Identify each of the following sentences by the number of the sentence pattern it illustrates.

91. The teacher assigns students a variety of subjects to research.

92. Then students write their research papers.

93. Many college libraries today have computerized book catalogs.

94. They are called on-line catalogs.

95. Librarians give students instructions for using these catalogs.

96. These catalogs are more flexible than the older card catalogs.

97. Computerized periodical indices also exist.

98. One CD-ROM can store many volumes of a periodical.

99. Most CD-ROMs contain issues only from recent years.

100. Thus, using the *Reader's Guide to Periodical Literature* is still necessary to find older materials.

 # Check Yourself

1. IM: instruction (**Types of sentences classified by purpose**)

2. IN: question (**Types of sentences classified by purpose**)

3. D: statement (**Types of sentences classified by purpose**)

4. IM: command (**Types of sentences classified by purpose**)

5. IM: command (**Types of sentences classified by purpose**)

6. D: statement (**Types of sentences classified by purpose**)

7. IN: question (**Types of sentences classified by purpose**)

8. E: strong emotion (**Types of sentences classified by purpose**)

9. D: statement (**Types of sentences classified by purpose**)

10. IM: instruction (**Types of sentences classified by purpose**)

11. simple subject: One; simple predicate. Verb: was (**Subjects and predicates**)

12. compound subject: his family and he; simple predicate. Verb: moved (**Subjects and predicates**)

13. simple subject: he; compound predicate. Verbs: practiced and perfected (**Subjects and predicates**)

14. simple subject: he; simple predicate. Verb: became (**Subjects and predicates**)

15. simple subject: he; simple predicate. Verb: was (**Subjects and predicates**)

16. compound subject: Escaping from ropes and freeing himself from handcuffs; simple predicate. Verb: amazed (**Subjects and predicates**)

17. simple subject: One; simple predicate. Verb: was (**Subjects and predicates**)

18. simple subject: he; simple predicate. Verb: escaped (**Subjects and predicates**)

19. simple subject: people; compound predicate. Verbs: watched and applauded (**Subjects and predicates**)

20. simple subject: he; simple predicate. Verb: freed (**Subjects and predicates**)

21. D (**Independent and dependent clauses**)

22. D (**Independent and dependent clauses**)

23. I (**Independent and dependent clauses**)

24. I (**Independent and dependent clauses**)

25. I **(Independent and dependent clauses)**

26. D **(Independent and dependent clauses)**

27. D **(Independent and dependent clauses)**

28. I **(Independent and dependent clauses)**

29. D **(Independent and dependent clauses)**

30. I **(Independent and dependent clauses)**

31. S **(Independent and dependent clauses)**

32. CX: *which struck Southern California on January 17, 1994* is a dependent clause. **(Types of sentences classified by clause structure)**

33. CD: two independent clauses joined by *"and"* **(Types of sentences classified by clause structure)**

34. CC: *When tornado warnings appear* is a dependent clause. It is followed by two independent clauses joined by *and.* **(Types of sentences classified by clause structure)**

35. CD: two independent clauses joined by *but* **(Types of sentences classified by clause structure)**

36. S **(Types of sentences classified by clause structure)**

37. CX: *when an earthquake strik*es" is a dependent clause. **(Types of sentences classified by clause structure)**

38. S **(Types of sentences classified by clause structure)**

39. CD: two independent clauses joined by *but* **(Types of sentences classified by clause structure)**

40. CX: *Whenever disasters occur* is a dependent clause. **(Types of sentences classified by clause structure)**

41. CC: independent clause, dependent clause *while both describe regional culture,* independent clause **(Types of sentences classified by clause structure)**

42. CD: two independent clauses joined by *but* **(Types of sentences classified by clause structure)**

43. CX: *When Hollywood makes disaster movies* is a dependent clause. **(Types of sentences classified by clause structure)**

44. S **(Types of sentences classified by clause structure)**

45. CD: two independent clauses joined by *and* **(Types of sentences classified by clause structure)**

46. CX: *Because the disease has no cure* is a dependent clause. **(Types of sentences classified by clause structure)**

47. S **(Types of sentences classified by clause structure)**

48. CX: *When a great fire destroyed much of London in 1666* is a dependent clause. **(Types of sentences classified by clause structure)**

49. CD two independent clauses joined by *and* **(Types of sentences classified by clause structure)**

50. S (**Types of sentences classified by clause structure**)

51. E. B. White's essay "Once More to the Lake" is a classic, and many generations of readers have enjoyed it. (**Correcting fused sentences and comma splices**)

52. correct (**Correcting fused sentences and comma splices**)

53. White notes changes in the vacation experience; however, he finds its essence is unchanged. (**Correcting fused sentences and comma splices**)

54. correct (**Correcting fused sentences and comma splices**)

55. Concrete and specific details fill the essay, yet its theme is an abstraction, the sense of mortality. (**Correcting fused sentences and comma splices**)

56. Some families enjoy vacationing at a lake; others prefer to go to an ocean beach. (**Correcting fused sentences and comma splices**)

57. Carol's family vacations by camping, or they may hike in a national park. (**Correcting fused sentences and comma splices**)

58. On her vacation, Natasha went to Santa Fe, New Mexico; consequently, she was able to attend both the Santa Fe Opera and the Santa Fe Chamber Music Festival. (**Correcting fused sentences and comma splices**)

59. Native Americans live in the pueblo in Taos, New Mexico, and they worship in the pueblo's ancient church. (**Correcting fused sentences and comma splices**)

60. correct (**Correcting fused sentences and comma splices**)

61. Disney provides Americans with two vacation spots: Disneyland is in Anaheim, California; and Disney World in Orlando, Florida. (**Correcting fused sentences and comma splices**)

62. Some people think that New York City is a nice place to visit, but they would not want to live there. (**Correcting fused sentences and comma splices**)

63. New Yorkers suffer many inconveniences; however, many feel the city's rewards make the effort of daily living worthwhile. (**Correcting fused sentences and comma splices**)

64. Joan Didion's writing portrays the essence of cities; she has written about Las Vegas, Miami, Los Angeles, and New York. (**Correcting fused sentences and comma splices**)

65. correct. (**Correcting fused sentences and comma splices**)

66. The National Aeronautics and Space Museum is extremely popular; it is part of the Smithsonian Institution. (**Correcting fused sentences and comma splices**)

67. Denver's altitude is high; consequently, baseballs hit at Coors Park travel farther than they would if hit at a sea-level ballpark like County Stadium in Milwaukee. (**Correcting fused sentences and comma splices**)

68. correct (**Correcting fused sentences and comma splices**)

69. Similarly, in New York, Yankee fans don't root for the Mets, and Mets fans don't go to Yankee Stadium. (**Correcting fused sentences and comma splices**)

70. In 1995, Hideo Nomo became a pitcher for the Los Angeles Dodgers; he is the first Japanese person to play on an American major league team. (**Correcting fused sentences and comma splices**)

71-80.

Anne's hobby is restoring old furniture. She works on useful items like chairs, tables, and desks to earn extra money. A leg on a kitchen chair was loose. Using some new wood, she made a replacement leg. After sanding the leg and carefully and neatly varnishing it, she finished the job. Because the chair was safer as well as more attractive, whoever bought the chair would be getting a good piece of furniture. (There are other possible ways to correct the errors.) (**Correcting sentence fragments**)

81-90.

The Statue of Liberty was dedicated in New York in 1886. It was a gift from the French people, who contributed funds for its construction in Paris. It commemorates the friendship of the people of France and the people of the United States. It was made of hundreds of copper sheets hammered into shape by hand. After it was finished, it was disassembled and shipped to New York. Liberty holds a torch in her right hand, and on her head is a crown with seven spokes. (There are other possible ways to correct the errors.) (**Correcting sentence fragments**)

91. 4 (**Identifying sentence patterns**)

92. 2 (**Identifying sentence patterns**)

93. 2 (**Identifying sentence patterns**)

94. 2 (**Identifying sentence patterns**)

95. 4 (**Identifying sentence patterns**)

96. 5 (**Identifying sentence patterns**)

97. 1 (**Identifying sentence patterns**)

98. 2 (**Identifying sentence patterns**)

99. 3 (**Identifying sentence patterns**)

100. 5 (**Identifying sentence patterns**)

Grade Yourself

Circle the numbers of the questions you missed, then fill in the total incorrect for each topic. If you answered more than three questions incorrectly, you need to focus on that topic. (If a topic has less than three questions and you had at least one wrong, we suggest you study that topic also. Read your textbook, a review book, or ask your teacher for help.)

Subject: Sentence Basics

Topic	Question Numbers	Number Incorrect
Types of sentences classified by purpose	1, 2, 3, 4, 5, 6, 7, 8, 9, 10	
Subjects and predicates	11, 12, 13, 14, 15, 16, 17, 18, 19, 20	
Independent and dependent clauses	21, 22, 23, 24, 25, 26, 27, 28, 29, 30, 31	
Types of sentences classified by clause structure	32, 33, 34, 35, 36, 37, 38, 39, 40, 41, 42, 43, 44, 45, 46, 47, 48, 49, 50	
Correcting fused sentences and comma splices	51, 52, 53, 54, 55, 56, 57, 58, 59, 60, 61, 62, 63, 64, 65, 66, 67, 68, 69, 70	
Correcting sentence fragments	71, 72, 73, 74, 75, 76, 77, 78, 79, 80, 81, 82, 83, 84, 85, 86, 87, 88, 89, 90	
Identifying sentence patterns	91, 92, 93, 94, 95, 96, 97, 98, 99, 100	

Nouns and Articles

Test Yourself

2.1 Types of Nouns

Common nouns name classes of persons, places, things, quantities, actions, or ideas.

Examples:

 sister, city, number, game, wisdom

Proper nouns name a specific member of the class, and they always begin with a capital letter.

Examples:

 Ellen, Milwaukee, Kleenex, Parcheesi

Count nouns name items that can be counted.

Examples:

 sister, city, game

Mass nouns name items that cannot be counted, such as qualities, ideas, or bulk materials.

Examples:

 wisdom, socialism, flour

Collective nouns refer to a group that has more than one member.

Examples:

 team, jury

Compound nouns are formed by joining two or more words; the resulting word functions as a single noun.

Examples:

 post office, cowhand

The item a noun refers to is called its referent. Referents that can be perceived by the senses are named by *concrete nouns*.

Examples:

 dog, poodle, Fifi

Qualities and ideas are named by *abstract nouns*.

Examples:

 wisdom, gentility, socialism

A noun can be described by more than one of these names of kinds of nouns.

Identify the underlined noun in the following sentences as common or proper.

1. In <u>China</u>, there is a belief that posits a relationship between the design of a building and the good or ill fortune of its inhabitants.

2. This <u>belief</u> is called "feng shui."

3. It is believed that if the front door and back door of a building are directly across from each other, <u>energy</u> will flow out of the house.

4. <u>Bill Leung</u> would not buy a house that had the doors in line with each other.

5. Some <u>Russians</u> consider it good luck to bring bread and salt into a new home.

6. <u>Superstition</u> may have some basis in fact.

7. Suppose a <u>person</u> left a ladder open, with a can of paint on its shelf.

8. If you walked under the <u>ladder</u> and jostled it, paint could spill on you.

9. <u>Mirrors</u> that break produce potentially harmful shards of glass.

10. To be injured by cut <u>glass</u> would certainly be bad luck.

Identify the underlined nouns in the following sentences as count, mass, collective, or compound.

11. My new <u>video recorder</u> is easier to program than my old one was.

12. Some people refer to the remote-control device for their television set as a <u>clicker</u>.

13. The <u>studio audience</u> laughed loudly during the taping of the show.

14. The <u>crew</u> that taped the show was less amused.

15. They were bored by the star's corny sense of <u>humor</u>.

16. Can you remember when almost all television <u>programs</u> were live broadcasts?

17. Now almost every <u>show</u> is taped.

18. <u>Spontaneity</u> is a rare quality on television.

19. Many shows are written by a <u>team</u> of writers.

20. The individual's distinct <u>voice</u> is sometimes not heard.

Identify the underlined noun in the following sentences as abstract or concrete.

21. The Declaration of Independence states men have "certain inalienable <u>rights</u>."

22. "Among these are life, liberty, and the pursuit of <u>happiness</u>."

23. "Among" suggests that other rights are also inalienable; an early draft of the document suggested <u>property</u> was such a right.

24. Jefferson complained that King George III had quartered "large bodies of armed <u>troops</u>" among the colonists.

25. The <u>rifles</u> used by the colonists were less accurate than modern guns.

26. Elizabeth Cady Stanton's "Declaration of Sentiments and Resolutions," written in 1848, is a <u>declaration</u> of rights for women.

27. It complains of <u>injustices</u> suffered by women.

28. For example, women were not admitted to <u>colleges</u>.

29. Stanton writes that man never permitted woman "to exercise her inalienable right to the elective <u>franchise</u>."

30. Women in the mid-nineteenth century often wore <u>bonnets</u>.

2.2 Functions of Nouns in Sentences

A noun used as the subject of a verb is the *simple subject.* If two or more nouns are used, they are a *compound subject.* A complete subject is the entire noun phrase or noun clause as the verb's subject.

Nouns can also serve as direct or indirect objects of verbs and as objects of prepositions. In the sentence "Harry gave Helen the book," *book* is the direct object of the verb *gave,* and *Helen* is the indirect object of the verb *gave.* In the sentence "Helen returned the book to Harry," *Harry* is the object of the preposition *to*.

Nouns that follow linking verbs are called *subject complements*. In the sentence "Harry is a magician," *magician* is the subject complement of *Harry*.

Nouns that follow direct objects are *object complements*. In the sentence "Helen considers the puzzles an interesting challenge," *challenge* is the object complement of *puzzles*.

A noun or noun phrase immediately following a noun and renaming or identifying the same person or thing is an *appositive*. In the sentence "Harry Houdini, a magician, escaped from locked chests" *a magician* is an appositive identifying Harry Houdini.

In the following sentences, identify the underlined noun or noun phrase as a subject, object, complement, or appositive.

31. *Native Son*, by Richard Wright, is a <u>novel set in Chicago.</u>

32. Bigger Thomas, the <u>main character</u>, is a young black man who is victimized by whites.

33. Wright's autobiography, *Black Boy*, describes his <u>childhood</u> in the Deep South.

34. In 1947, Wright moved to <u>Paris</u>, where he remained until his death, in 1960.

35. <u>James Baldwin and Ralph Ellison</u> were two of the writers influenced by Wright.

36. Some critics think Baldwin's nonfiction is superior to his <u>novels.</u>

37. *Go Tell It on the Mountain*, an <u>autobiographical work</u>, was Baldwin's first novel.

38. It is difficult to classify Sandra Cisnero's *The House on Mango Street* as <u>poetry or prose</u>.

39. Ellen gave <u>the book</u> to Cousin Jan.

40. Cousin Jan gave <u>Aunt Maria</u> the book.

41. Everyone in the family enjoyed <u>the stories</u>.

42. Steve was impressed by the <u>film version</u> of Amy Tan's *The Joy Luck Club*.

43. <u>Maxine Hong Kingston's autobiographical *The Woman Warrior*</u> is a complex novel.

44. When adapted for the stage, it was not a <u>success</u>.

45. Philip Roth and Saul Bellow, <u>prominent Jewish-American authors,</u> write in very different styles.

46. Chief Joseph told his <u>listeners</u> he would fight no more.

47. <u>Magic realism</u> is the name given to the style used by Gabriel García Marquez.

48. S. Y. Agnon, who lived in Europe and Israel, won the <u>Nobel Prize</u> in literature.

49. When President Kennedy was inaugurated, he selected Robert Frost to read a poem at the <u>ceremony</u>.

50. Maya Angelou wrote a poem specifically for <u>President Clinton's inauguration</u>.

2.3 Identifying Noun Phrases and Noun Clauses

A *noun phrase* consists of a noun and additional words modifying the noun, but it does not contain a verb.

A *noun clause* is a group of words that serves the function of a noun in a sentence. It may or may not contain a noun. Since it is a clause, it will contain a verb.

In the following sentences, identify the underlined group of words as a noun phrase or as a noun clause.

51. In 1995, <u>the British Open Golf Championship</u> was played at St. Andrews in Scotland.

52. The winner of the British Open was John Daly, <u>the first American to win</u> since 1989.

53. Corey Pavin won the United States Open Golf Championship, <u>which was played at Shinnecock Hills on Long Island.</u>

54. <u>Professional golfer Nancy Lopez</u> has had great success on the women's golf tour.

55. <u>Whatever success golfers have</u> is a result of practice, patience, and luck.

56. <u>The PGA Seniors Tour</u> features golfers who are over fifty years old.

57. Prominent golfers on the Senior Tour include <u>the ageless Arnold Palmer</u>, Jack Nicklaus, and Lee Trevino.

58. The great distance <u>that John Daly drives a golf ball</u> thrills spectators.

59. If there were a senior tour for women golfers, <u>popular favorite Joanne Carner</u> would probably be one of its stars.

60. Chi Chi Rodriguez is known not only for his golf but also for his <u>many charities that benefit children.</u>

2.4 Forming Plurals of Nouns

Most nouns form plurals by adding "s."

Nouns ending in "ch," "sh," "x," and "z" add "es."

If a noun ends in a consonant followed by "y," change "y" to "i" and add "es." If there is a vowel before the "y," add "s."

Some nouns have irregular plurals because they are taken directly from languages other than English, or

the plural form may be retained from an early stage of the English language.

Examples:

    medium (singular)/media (plural)

    index (singular)/indices (plural)

    goose (singular)/geese (plural)

    mouse (singular)/mice (plural)

The noun in parentheses in each of the following sentences is singular. Change each to the correct plural form.

61. What are the (basis) for thinking life may exist on other planets?

62. So far, (astronomer) have not seen evidence of life outside the solar system.

63. Sven stored his files in several large (box).

64. The relationships of several (family) surnamed Olson were shown in the genealogy chart.

65. Ibsen's (play) *Hedda Gabler* and *A Doll's House* are about women's position in society.

66. Several different (company) offer access to the Internet.

67. Do you think information on the Internet is part of the broadcast (medium)?

68. "Ouch," Sam yelped, as the (mosquito) bit him.

69. How many (turkey) do you think are eaten in the United States on Thanksgiving Day?

70. Seven (class) of seniors have graduated from Oakmont High since the school opened.

2.5 Forming Possessives of Nouns

To form the possessive of a noun that does not end in "s," add "'s." This is true whether the noun is singular or plural.

Examples:

the baby's diaper, the children's gloves

To form the possessive of a singular noun that ends in "s," add "'s" or only "'." Both are acceptable.

Example:

the boss's desk or the boss' desk.

If a plural noun ends in "s," add only "'."

Example:

The elephants' trunks

In the following sentences, change the noun in parentheses to the possessive form.

71. Grand Stores are showing the (season) newest fashions.

72. The styles are hard to wear; let's change the (designers) attitudes.

73. The skirts come in junior and (women) sizes.

74. (Girls) shoes are available in sizes one through four.

75. The Garcias are buying the (Smith) house.

76. The (Jones) house is also for sale.

77. Kimberly is working in her (dad) printshop.

78. Today many (jobs) requirements include computer literacy.

79. Robertson is playing left field in (Saturday) baseball game.

80. It is not legal to put cork in a baseball (bat) handle.

81. Al Davis, the (Raiders) owner, is moving the team to Oakland.

82. The Harley is (Joy) motorcycle.

83. All of my (friends) cars are newer than mine.

84. (James) car is illegally parked.

85. At the Country Cafe, biscuits and gravy is (today) special.

86. The (wrestlers) bodies seemed to hit so hard that the spectators winced.

87. Who can ever forget (Elvis) voice?

88. The (families) heirlooms are stored in the attic.

89. At Old Harbor the (wharves) timbers are rotting.

90. Completing a (day) work provides me with a sense of satisfaction.

2.6 Using Articles

The is used with most nouns whose specific identity is known to the reader from the passage.

A or *an* is used before nouns when a specific member of the category the noun refers to is unknown. Use *a* before consonant sounds; use *an* before vowel sounds.

Use *a*, *an*, or *the* with singular count nouns.

Examples:

a city, an egg, the game

Use only *the* with plural count nouns.

Examples:

the cities, the eggs, the games

Use only *the* or no article with mass nouns.

Examples:

Measure the flour carefully. Achieve [no article] wisdom through contemplation.

Fill in the following blanks with *a*, *an*, or *the*, or leave them blank to complete the sentence correctly.

91. Entomology is _____ study of insects.

92. _____ etymologist studies the history of words.

93. _____ physiology describes the functions of the parts of living organisms.

94. Phrenology was _____ pseudoscience that claimed to describe character based on the shape of one's skull.

95. "It's _____ honor to be here," the speaker said.

96. "Thank you for _____ invitation to address you."

97. "This is _____ great occasion for me."

98. "I don't claim to know all _____ answers to your questions."

99. "Ladies and gentlemen, let's give our speaker _____ big hand."

100. The bored audience noted that _____ speaker had expressed many trite sentiments.

✓ Check Yourself

1. proper (**Types of nouns**)

2. common (**Types of nouns**)

3. common (**Types of nouns**)

4. proper (**Types of nouns**)

5. proper (**Types of nouns**)

6. common (**Types of nouns**)

7. common (**Types of nouns**)

8. common (**Types of nouns**)

9. common (**Types of nouns**)

10. common (**Types of nouns**)

11. compound (**Types of nouns**)

12. count (**Types of nouns**)

13. compound (**Types of nouns**)

14. collective (**Types of nouns**)

15. mass (**Types of nouns**)

16. count (**Types of nouns**)

17. count (**Types of nouns**)

18. mass (**Types of nouns**)

19. collective (**Types of nouns**)

20. count (**Types of nouns**)

21. abstract (**Types of nouns**)

22. abstract (**Types of nouns**)

23. concrete (**Types of nouns**)

24. concrete (**Types of nouns**)

25. concrete (**Types of nouns**)

26. concrete (**Types of nouns**)

27. abstract (**Types of nouns**)

28. concrete (**Types of nouns**)

29. abstract (**Types of nouns**)

30. concrete (**Types of nouns**)

31. complement: follows linking verb *is* (**Functions of nouns in sentences**)

32. appositive: identifies *Bigger Thomas* (**Functions of nouns in sentences**)

33. object: of the verb *describes* (**Functions of nouns in sentences**)

34. object: of preposition *to* (**Functions of nouns in sentences**)

35. subject (**Functions of nouns in sentences**)

36. object: of preposition *to* (**Functions of nouns in sentences**)

37. appositive: describes *Go Tell It on the Mountain* (**Functions of nouns in sentences**)

38. object: of preposition *as* (**Functions of nouns in sentences**)

39. object: of verb *gave* (**Functions of nouns in sentences**)

40. object (indirect): of *gave* (**Functions of nouns in sentences**)

41. object: of verb *enjoyed* (**Functions of nouns in sentences**)

42. object: of preposition *by* (**Functions of nouns in sentences**)

43. subject (**Functions of nouns in sentences**)

44. complement: of linking verb *was* (**Functions of nouns in sentences**)

45. appositive: describes *Philip Roth and Saul Bellow* (**Functions of nouns in sentences**)

46. object (indirect): of *told* (**Functions of nouns in sentences**)

47. subject (**Functions of nouns in sentences**)

48. object: of verb *won* (**Functions of nouns in sentences**)

49. object: of preposition *at* (**Functions of nouns in sentences**)

50. object: of preposition *for* (**Functions of nouns in sentences**)

51. phrase (**Noun phrases and noun clauses**)

52. phrase (**Noun phrases and noun clauses**)

53. clause (**Noun phrases and noun clauses**)

54. phrase (**Noun phrases and noun clauses**)

55. clause (**Noun phrases and noun clauses**)

56. phrase (**Noun phrases and noun clauses**)

57. phrase (**Noun phrases and noun clauses**)

58. clause (**Noun phrases and noun clauses**)

59. phrase (**Noun phrases and noun clauses**)

60. clause (**Noun phrases and noun clauses**)

61. bases (**Forming plurals of nouns**)

62. astronomers (**Forming plurals of nouns**)

63. boxes (**Forming plurals of nouns**)

64. families (**Forming plurals of nouns**)

65. plays (**Forming plurals of nouns**)

66. companies (**Forming plurals of nouns**)

67. media (**Forming plurals of nouns**)

68. mosquitoes (**Forming plurals of nouns**)

69. turkeys (**Forming plurals of nouns**)

70. classes (**Forming plurals of nouns**)

71. season's (**Forming possessives of nouns**)

72. designers' (**Forming possessives of nouns**)

73. women's (**Forming possessives of nouns**)

74. Girls' (**Forming possessives of nouns**)

75. Smiths' (**Forming possessive of nouns**)

76. Jones's or Joneses' (**Forming possessives of nouns**)

77. dad's (**Forming possessives of nouns**)

78. jobs' (**Forming possessives of nouns**)

79. Saturday's (**Forming possessives of nouns**)

80. bat's (**Forming possessives of nouns**)

81. Raiders' (**Forming possessives of nouns**)

82. Joy's (**Forming possessives of nouns**)

83. friends' (**Forming possessives of nouns**)

84. James' or James's (**Forming possessives of nouns**)

85. today's (**Forming possessives of nouns**)

86. wrestlers' (**Forming possessives of nouns**)

87. Elvis' or Elvis's (**Forming possessives of nouns**)

88. families' (**Forming possessives of nouns**)

89. wharves' (**Forming possessives of nouns**)

90. day's (**Forming possessives of nouns**)

91. the (**Using articles**)

92. an (**Using articles**)

93. leave blank (**Using articles**)

94. a (**Using articles**)

95. an (**Using articles**)

96. the (**Using articles**)

97. a (**Using articles**)

98. the (**Using articles**)

99. a (**Using articles**)

100. the (**Using articles**)

Grade Yourself

Circle the numbers of the questions you missed, then fill in the total incorrect for each topic. If you answered more than three questions incorrectly, you need to focus on that topic. (If a topic has less than three questions and you had at least one wrong, we suggest you study that topic also. Read your textbook, a review book, or ask your teacher for help.)

Subject: Nouns and Articles

Topic	Question Numbers	Number Incorrect
Types of nouns	1, 2, 3, 4, 5, 6, 7, 8, 9, 10, 11, 12, 13, 14, 15, 16, 17, 18, 19, 20, 21, 22, 23, 24, 25, 26, 27, 28, 29, 30	
Functions of nouns in sentences	31, 32, 33, 34, 35, 36, 37, 38, 39, 40, 41, 42, 43, 44, 45, 46, 47, 48, 49, 50	
Noun phrases and noun clauses	51, 52, 53, 54, 55, 56, 57, 58, 59, 60	
Forming plurals of nouns	61, 62, 63, 64, 65, 66, 67, 68, 69, 70	
Forming possessives of nouns	71, 72, 73, 74, 75, 76, 77, 78, 79, 80, 81, 82, 83, 84, 85, 86, 87, 88, 89, 90	
Using articles	91, 92, 93, 94, 95, 96, 97, 98, 99, 100	

Pronouns

3

  Test Yourself

3.1 Personal Pronouns

Personal pronouns can be in the subject or object case. The subject personal pronouns are *I*, *you*, *he*, *she*, *it*, *we*, *you*, and *they*. The object personal pronouns are *me*, *you*, *him*, *her*, *it*, *us*, *you*, and *them*.

Pronouns must agree with their antecedents in number. Singular antecedents require singular pronouns; plural antecedents require plural pronouns. Collective nouns usually take singular pronouns.

Example:

> The faculty of the college stated its position on student fees.

The faculty is treated as one group. But if the persons in the group are thought of as acting individually, use a plural pronoun.

Example:

> The faculty debated their positions.

The faculty members are treated as individuals. When a singular and plural antecedent are linked by "either/or" or "neither/nor," the pronoun should agree with the antecedent that is closest to it in the sentence.

Examples:

> Either the group leader or the students will present their petition not to raise student fees to the board of trustees.
> Neither the students nor the faculty will change its position.

Pronouns must agree with their antecedents in gender. However, if the antecedent may be male or female, avoid using a masculine or feminine pronoun. Rewrite the sentence so that the antecedent is plural, or use both masculine and feminine singular pronouns, or eliminate the personal pronoun. Non-human creatures as antecedents take a neuter pronoun, unless the gender of the antecedent is clear from the context.

Example:

> "The installation ceremony for a new judge is called his 'enrobing'" assumes that all judges are men. Appropriate revisions include "The installation ceremony for new judges is called 'enrobing'"; or "The installation ceremony for a new judge is called his or her 'enrobing'"; or "The installation ceremony for a new judge is called 'enrobing.'"

Personal pronouns in the possessive case (my, mine, your, yours, our, ours, your, yours, their, theirs) do not use apostrophes to indicate possession.

Identify the pronoun that correctly completes each of the following sentences.

1. My friend and (I/me) don't have much time to eat lunch.

2. (We/Us) two usually go to a fast food place.

3. Sometimes we divide a large order of fries between him and (I/me).

4. Sal's friend and (he/him) like pepperoni pizza.

5. Advertisement: Blatt Cellular phones make communication simpler for you and (I/me).

6. Henry asked Al and (I/me) to go to the computer store with him.

7. (He/Him) and his brother want to buy a new printer.

8. Anna's sister is ten years older than (she/her).

9. (She/Her) and her sister were both born in August.

10. Ned doesn't think astrological signs have any influence on (he/him).

If the pronoun in the following sentences agrees in number with its antecedent, write A. If the pronoun and antecedent do not agree, write the correct pronoun.

11. Although fast food is cheap and convenient, they may contain large amounts of fat.

12. Neither Captain Kirk nor the other crew members were aware of their peril.

13. On the *Starship Enterprise*, the members of the crew recognized its duties and obligations.

14. In the film *Rashomon*, the narrator of each story places blame for the murder on a different person, and they try to look innocent.

15. For these characters, preservation of their honor is crucial.

16. When the witness's testimony became boring, the jury stared at their feet.

17. Some people argue that men are paid more than women because he has a family to support.

18. The largest of the cetaceans is the sperm whale; they may weigh several tons.

19. When we look at one of these huge creatures, it may seem awkward.

20. Either Ann's dogs or her cat can respond to its name.

Rewrite the following sentences to eliminate inappropriate gender references.

21. Dr. Gonzalez, a veterinarian, has her office on Seventh Street.

22. When bathing a pet, try to keep soap out of his eyes.

23. The letter carrier parked his truck at the corner.

24. The postal supervisor is responsible for the delivery of mail in her district.

25. Every stamp collector has her favorite among new issues.

26. If a person works too hard, he is likely to feel emotional stress.

27. A good teacher makes sure his students understand instructions.

28. As we were watching the bear emerge from the den, she suddenly growled.

29. A politician should not accept financial contributions meant to change her vote.

30. Each state senator has his own office staff.

In the following sentences, insert an apostrophe in the personal pronoun if it is part of a contraction; if the personal pronoun is possessive, do not change it.

31. Queen City is proud of its history.

32. Its too early to leave for the fireworks show, which doesn't start until dark.

33. Kim and Loo want to leave now; theyre anxious to find a place to park.

34. They will bring their lawn chairs with them to the park.

35. When you arrive, follow the instructions about where to park your car.

36. If you do not, youre going to be cited for a parking violations.

37. The fireworks illuminated the night sky with their many colors.

38. The colors of the Roman candle burst forth a few seconds after the spectators heard its explosion.

39. If youre using fireworks, be sure to follow all safety instructions.

40. Theyre very dangerous if not handled properly.

3.2 Reflexive Pronouns

The reflexive pronouns are *myself, yourself, himself, herself, itself, oneself, ourselves, yourselves,* and *themselves.*

Do not use reflexive pronouns as the subjects of sentences.

Example:

"My study group and myself will meet on Thursday" is incorrect because *myself* is used as the subject of *will meet.* The sentence should read "My study group and I will meet on Thursday."

Do not use a reflexive pronoun in a prepositional phrase unless it refers to a person or thing mentioned earlier in the sentence.

Examples:

"The doctor reserved the appointment time for myself" is incorrect, because *myself* is part of the prepositional phrase *for myself.* In the sentence "I went to the doctor by myself even though I was so ill I could hardly drive a car," *myself* is correct because it refers to *I.*

Reflexive pronouns may be used as intensifiers or to create emphasis.

Example:

The students themselves chose a subject for their sociology project.

In the following sentences, if the reflexive pronoun is used correctly, write R. If it is not used correctly, write N.

41. Helena Montgomery, an attorney, said, "I've set up a meeting between my client and myself for later this week."

42. Ms. Montgomery did the research for the meeting by herself.

43. Computerized research was easy for herself.

44. The computer search itself produced many cases to cite.

45. It was more difficult to do research when one had to use the case books by themselves.

46. Dan Buckley and myself took classes to learn how to use a computer for legal research.

47. Dan thought to himself, "I wish I'd known about this program sooner."

48. Judge Crito, the defendant's lawyer, and myself were present at a settlement conference.

49. Ms. Montgomery told her client, "Just between ourselves, I don't think this case will settle."

50. "Yourself and the defendant have too many disagreements," she added.

3.3 Relative Pronouns

Relative pronouns introduce dependent clauses in sentences. *That* or *which* may be used to introduce restrictive clauses. Use only *which* to introduce non-restrictive clauses.

Example:

The buses on Line 789, [that or which] were painted green, went from Broad Street to

Seventh Avenue. The seats which were in the front of the bus were reserved.

When a relative pronoun is the subject of its clause, use *who* or *whoever*. When it is an object, use *whom* or *whomever*.

Although *that* may be used for both people and things, it is preferable to use *who* for people and *that* or *which* for things.

Examples:

Rosa Parks is the woman who refused to give up her seat on a bus. The bus that runs on Broadway was late this morning.

Identify the word that correctly completes each of the following sentences.

51. The instructor was annoyed with the students (that/who) didn't read the assignment.

52. "You are the ones (that/who) will need the information," he said.

53. Our text, (that/which) explains fundamentals of grammar, is not complicated.

54. Students (who/whom) did not do the assignment complained that it was boring.

55. (Whoever/Whomever) I see revising carefully is doing the assignment correctly.

56. The answer was explained by Sarah Blake, (who/whom) had done the assignment.

57. Mel Jones is the animal control officer (that/who) patrols the neighborhood.

58. Jones asked the neighbors (who/whom) was the owner of the dog.

59. "To (who/whom) does this dog belong?"

60. (Whoever/Whomever) the owner was did not claim the dog from the animal shelter.

3.4 Interrogative Pronouns

Use *who* and *whoever* in questions as subjects of verbs.

Use *whom* and *whomever* in questions as objects of verbs and prepositions.

Identify the word that correctly completes each of the following questions.

61. "From (who/whom) did you receive that shirt as a gift?" asked Letty.

62. (Who/Whom) has such a poor sense of color?

63. (Whoever/Whomever) would buy such an ugly thing?

64. (Whom/Who) did you insult by asking such a question?

65. With (who/whom) did you go shopping?

66. (Who/Whom) chose the new jeans, you or your brother?

67. "You bought the jeans from (who/whom)?" I asked.

68. "(Who/Whom) is the manufacturer of the best-fitting jeans?" asked Lou.

69. "That depends. (Who/Whom) is wearing them?" Sylvia replied.

70. Of (who/whom) are you speaking when you say Exotica jeans fit best?

3.5 Indefinite Pronouns

Although indefinite pronouns such as *each*, *everyone*, *neither*, and *somebody* seem to have plural meanings, they are singular grammatically.

Indefinite pronouns such as *both* and *many* are always plural.

> Indefinite pronouns such as *all*, *any*, and *some* may be singular or plural, depending on the context of the sentence.

Rewrite the following sentences to correct any errors caused by failure of an antecedent or verb to agree with the indefinite pronoun.

71. Neither of us have ever gone camping before.

72. Every camper told a story that described their family.

73. None of the campers are too tired to stay up for the weenie roast.

74. All of the campers became skilled in pitching his or her tent.

75. The group leader made sure each of the campers took their turn at cleaning up the area.

76. Each of those delicious french fries are full of fat.

77. When you love someone, you should be kind to them

78. Everyone know what it's like to be stuck in traffic.

79. In Los Angeles, most of the freeways is jammed all day.

80. Either Pacific Coast Highway or Sepulveda Boulevard is a good alternate route.

3.6 Antecedents

Be sure there is an antecedent for a pronoun in the sentence or in the material close to the sentence. Do not use a pronoun so far away from the antecedent that the meaning is unclear.

Avoid using pronouns such as *this*, *that*, and *they*, which have vague or broad antecedents.

Change sentences in which the pronoun could refer to more than one antecedent.

If the following sentences are clear, write C. If they are unclear, write U.

81. In George Orwell's "Shooting an Elephant," it describes his situation when he was a police officer in Burma.

82. An elephant had gone on a rampage, but when Orwell saw it, the fit was over.

83. Orwell knew the elephant should not be killed, but they always say elephants can be dangerous.

84. After he shot the elephant, the villagers hacked up its carcass because they would use it as meat.

85. Orwell shot the elephant because he felt his role as an officer of the British police required him to do this.

86. Orwell's novel *1984* describes a tyrannical government. There is no privacy, history is rewritten to reflect current government policy, and the nation is constantly at war; this is a difficult situation.

87. In *Animal Farm*, domestic animals rebel against humans who have mistreated them.

88. The pigs Snowball and Napoleon are leaders, but his victory leads to dissension.

89. During the Spanish Civil War, Orwell fought against the Fascists in a militia group; this was consistent with his political views.

90. Although Orwell's predictions have not come true, that does not decrease his stature as a writer.

3.7 Avoiding Illogical Pronoun Shifts

In a sentence or passage, do not shift from one person to another or between singular and plural unless there is a specific reason to do so.

There are ten pronouns in the paragraph below. Correct any confusing pronoun shifts by changing the pronoun or rewriting the sentence.

91-100. When writing a paper, one should be aware that you are writing for an anticipated audience. Keep your reader in mind, and they will help shape the content and tone of the paper. For most college assignments, students should assume an audience of their peers; they are other students with similar backgrounds and knowledge. In advanced level courses, one may assume that your readers have more than general knowledge of a subject and that she or he does not need explanations of terms common to academic discourse.

 # Check Yourself

1. I: subject of the verb *do (not) have* (**Personal pronoun case**)

2. We: subject of the verb *will go* (**Personal pronoun case**)

3. me: object of the preposition *between* (**Personal pronoun case**)

4. he: subject of the verb *like* (**Personal pronoun case**)

5. me: object of the preposition *for* (**Personal pronoun case**)

6. me: object of the verb *asked* (**Personal pronoun case**)

7. He: subject of the verb *want* (**Personal pronoun case**)

8. she: subject of the implied verb *is* (**Personal pronoun case**)

9. She: subject of the verb *were* (**Personal pronoun case**)

10. him: object of the preposition *on* (**Personal pronoun case**)

11. it: *food* is the antecedent (**Agreement of pronouns and antecedents**)

12. A (**Agreement of pronouns and antecedents**)

13. their: *members of the crew* are acting as individuals (**Agreement of pronouns and antecedents**)

14. each tries: *narrator* is the antecedent (**Agreement of pronouns and antecedents**)

15. A (**Agreement of pronouns and antecedents**)

16. A: members of the jury look at their own feet (**Agreement of pronouns and antecedents**)

17. they have: *men* is the antecedent (**Agreement of pronouns and antecedents**)

18. it: *whale* is the antecedent (**Agreement of pronouns and antecedents**)

19. A (**Agreement of pronouns and antecedents**)

20. A: *cat* is the antecedent closest to the pronoun (**Agreement of pronouns and antecedents**)

21. Dr. Gonzalez, a veterinarian, has an office on Seventh Street. (**Gender of pronouns**)

22. When bathing a pet, try to keep soap out of its eyes. (**Gender of pronouns**)

23. The letter carrier's truck was parked at the corner. (**Gender of pronouns**)

24. Postal supervisors are responsible for the delivery of mail in their districts. (**Gender of pronouns**)

25. Every stamp collector has his or her favorite among new issues. (**Gender of pronouns**)

26. If a person works too hard, he or she is likely to feel stress. (**Gender of pronouns**)

27. Good teachers make sure their students understand instructions. (**Gender of pronouns**)

28. As we were watching the bear emerge from the den, it suddenly growled. (**Gender of pronouns**)

29. Politicians should not accept financial contributions meant to influence their votes. (**Gender of pronouns**)

30. State senators have their own office staffs. (**Gender of pronouns**)

31. no change (**Possessive pronouns and contractions**)

32. It's (**Possessive pronouns and contractions**)

33. They're (**Possessive pronouns and contractions**)

34. no change (**Possessive pronouns and contractions**)

35. no change (**Possessive pronouns and contractions**)

36. you're (**Possessive pronouns and contractions**)

37. no change (**Possessive pronouns and contractions**)

38. no change (**Possessive pronouns and contractions**)

39. you're (**Possessive pronouns and contractions**)

40. They're (**Possessive pronouns and contractions**)

41. N: *myself* is part of the prepositional phrase b*etween my client and myself.* The phrase should be *between my client and me.* (**Reflexive pronouns**)

42. R (**Reflexive pronouns**)

43. N: *herself* is part of the prepositional phrase *for herself.* The phrase should be *for her.* (**Reflexive pronouns**)

44. R (**Reflexive pronouns**)

45. R (**Reflexive pronouns**)

46. N: *myself* is part of the subject of the verb *took.* The sentence should read "Dan Buckley and I took classes to learn how to use a computer for legal research." (**Reflexive pronouns**)

47. R (**Reflexive pronouns**)

48. N: *myself* is part of the subject of the verb *were.* The sentence should read "Judge Crito, the defendant's lawyer, and I were present at a settlement conference." (**Reflexive pronouns**)

49. N: *ourselves* is part of the prepositional phrase *between ourselves*. The phrase should be "between us." **(Reflexive pronouns)**

50. N: *yourself* is part of the subject of the verb *have*. The sentence should read "You and the defendant have too many disagreements, she added." **(Reflexive pronouns)**

51. who: refers to *students* **(Relative pronouns)**

52. who: subject of *will need* **(Relative pronouns)**

53. which: introduces a nonrestrictive clause **(Relative pronouns)**

54. who: subject of *did (not) do* **(Relative pronouns)**

55. Whomever: object of *see* **(Relative pronouns)**

56. who: subject of *has done* **(Relative pronouns)**

57. who: Mel Jones is a person **(Relative pronouns)**

58. who: subject of *was* **(Relative pronouns)**

59. whom: object of the preposition *to* **(Relative pronouns)**

60. whoever: subject of *was* **(Relative pronouns)**

61. whom: object of *from* **(Interrogative pronouns)**

62. who: subject of *has* **(Interrogative pronouns)**

63. whoever: subject of *would buy* **(Interrogative pronouns)**

64. whom object of *did insult* **(Interrogative pronouns)**

65. Whom: object of *did go shopping* (interrogative pronoun)

66. Who: subject of *chose* **(Interrogative pronouns)**

67. whom: object of *for* **(Interrogative pronouns)**

68. Who: Subject of *is* **(Interrogative pronouns)**

69. Who: subject of "is" **(Interrogative pronouns)**

70. whom: object of *of* **(Interrogative pronouns)**

71. Neither of us has ever gone camping before. **(Indefinite pronouns)**

72. Every camper told a story that described his or her family. **(Indefinite pronouns)**

73. None of the campers is too tired to stay up for the weenie roast. **(Indefinite pronouns)**

74. All of the campers became skilled in pitching their tents. **(Indefinite pronouns)**

75. The group leader made sure each of the campers took his or her turn at cleaning up the area. **(Indefinite pronouns)**

76. Each of those delicious french fries is full of fat. **(Indefinite pronouns)**

77. When you love someone, you should be kind to him or her. **(Indefinite pronouns)**

78. Everyone knows what it's like to be stuck in traffic. **(Indefinite pronouns)**

79. In Los Angeles, all of the freeways are jammed most of the day. **(Indefinite pronouns)**

80. Either Pacific Coast Highway or Sepulveda Boulevard is a good alternate route. **(Indefinite pronouns)**

81. U: What does *it* refer to? **(Avoiding confusing antecedents)**

82. U: Does *it* refer to the elephant or to the rampage? **(Avoiding confusing antecedents)**

83. U: Who are *they*? **(Avoiding confusing antecedents)**

84. U: Does *it* refer to the elephant or to meat? **(Avoiding confusing antecedents)**

85. C **(Avoiding confusing antecedents)**

86. U: Does *this* refer to war or all of the conditions described? **(Avoiding confusing antecedents)**

87. C **(Avoiding confusing antecedents)**

88. U: Does *his* refer to Snowball or Napoleon, or both of them? **(Avoiding confusing antecedents)**

89. U: Does *this* refer to *against the Fascists* or *belonging to a militia group*? **(Avoiding confusing antecedents)**

90. C **(Avoiding confusing antecedents)**

91-100.

When writing an essay, one should be aware of writing for an anticipated audience. Keep the readers in mind, and this will help shape the content and tone of the paper. For most college assignments, students should assume an audience of their peers; they are other students with similar backgrounds and knowledge. In advanced-level courses, one may assume that the readers have more than general knowledge of a subject and that they do not need explanations of terms common to academic discourse. **(Avoiding pronoun shifts)**

Grade Yourself

Circle the numbers of the questions you missed, then fill in the total incorrect for each topic. If you answered more than three questions incorrectly, you need to focus on that topic. (If a topic has less than three questions and you had at least one wrong, we suggest you study that topic also. Read your textbook, a review book, or ask your teacher for help.)

Subject: Pronouns

Topic	Question Numbers	Number Incorrect
Personal pronoun case	1, 2, 3, 4, 5, 6, 7, 8, 9, 10	
Agreement of pronouns and antecedents	11, 12, 13, 14, 15, 16, 17, 18, 19, 20	
Gender of pronouns	21, 22, 23, 24, 25, 26, 27, 28, 29, 30	
Possessive pronouns and contractions	31, 32, 33, 34, 35, 36, 37, 38, 39, 40	
Reflexive pronouns	41, 42, 43, 44, 45, 46, 47, 48, 49, 50	
Relative Pronouns	51, 52, 53, 54, 55, 56, 57, 58, 59, 60	
Interrogative pronouns	61, 62, 63, 64, 65, 66, 67, 68, 69, 70	
Indefinite pronouns	71, 72, 73, 74, 75, 76, 77, 78, 79, 80	
Avoiding confusing antecedents	81, 82, 83, 84, 85, 86, 87, 88, 89, 90	
Avoiding pronoun shifts	91, 92, 93, 94, 95, 96, 97, 98, 99 100	

Verbs

4

 Test Yourself

4.1   Types of Verbs

Transitive verbs are followed by direct objects that complete their meaning.

Example:

> In the sentence "I like ice cream," *like* is a transitive verb because it requires a direct object to complete the meaning of the sentence.

Intransitive verbs are not followed by direct objects or by object complements.

Example:

> In the sentence "I smile," *smile* is an intransitive verb because the sentence's meaning is complete without an object.

Linking verbs such as *be*, *appear*, and *seem* are followed by subject complements.

Examples:

> "Jennifer is the host for the party." *Host* is the subject complement. "Jennifer seems nervous." *Nervous* is the subject complement. "Jennifer appeared tired after the party was over." *Tired* is the subject complement.

Auxiliary verbs are function words that always appear with another verb. Some auxiliary verbs such as *be* and *have* indicate tense and voice. In the sentence "He is smiling," *is* is the auxiliary verb indicating present tense. In the sentence "Ice cream was enjoyed by the guests at the party," *was* is the auxiliary verb indicating the verb is in the passive voice. Modal auxiliaries such as *can*, *may*, and *should* indicate attitudes such as ability, permission, and obligation.

An auxiliary verb combined with the present or past participle of the basic verb creates a verb phrase. A finite verb can be the main verb in a sentence. Non-finite verbs are present and past participles that form part of a verb phrase. In the sentence "Jennifer is dancing at her party," *is* is a finite verb because it could be the main verb in another sentence. *Dancing* is a nonfinite verb because it could not serve by itself as the main verb in a sentence.

Identify the verb in the following sentences and state if it is transitive or intransitive.

1. Teen Club is running the bingo game at the carnival.

2. The clown is running away from the tiny car.

3. Roller coasters careen around steep tracks.

4. The barker encourages the customers to step right up to play the game.

5. We eat hot dogs, corn, and cotton candy at the fair.

6. The animals to be shown will walk around the ring.

7. Prize animal win blue ribbons.

8. After a week, the prize vegetables begin wilting.

9. After winning first prize for her apple pie three years in a row, Ms. Hawkins retired from the competition.

10. When the Diamond Boys Softball team won the tournament for the fifth year in a row, the donor retired the trophy.

Identify the verb or verb phrase in each of the following sentences. Indicate if it is a linking verb or a verb phrase that contains an auxiliary.

11. Etta feels proud of her skill as a potter.

12. She has applied to Alfred University's School of Ceramic Design.

13. Alfred University is located in the western part of New York State.

14. "Pot" is a generic term for a clay sculptures as well as a functional item such as cup, vase, and plate.

15. "Throwing a pot" may refer to forming a pot on a wheel.

16. Pots can be glazed before firing.

17. Kilns are the ovens in which pots are fired.

18. Students in the School of Ceramic Design must take liberal arts courses in addition to design classes.

19. Professor Klitzke's History of Art class was one of Etta's favorite courses.

20. Etta will earn a Bachelor of Arts degree in four years.

4.2 Verb Tenses

For regular verbs, the principle parts are the basic form: the past tense, which is formed by adding *-ed* to the basic form; and the past participle, which is usually the past tense form preceded by a form of *have*. For irregular verbs, consult a dictionary or handbook to determine the correct principle parts.

The six verb tenses are:

present	I smile
past	I smiled
future	I will smile
present perfect	I have smiled *= past participle*
past perfect	I had smiled
future perfect	I will have smiled

The progressive forms of these tenses combine an auxiliary verb with the verb's present participle. Progressive forms describe actions that continue, were continuing, or will continue.

Examples:

I am smiling. I will be smiling.

Do not shift tenses of verbs within a passage unless there is a reason to do so. When actions occur in different time frames, choose verb tenses that clearly indicate the order of actions.

In the following sentences, insert the past or past participle form for the basic verb as indicated in the parentheses.

21. Because Hassan was tired, he (past-sleep) well.

22. Milo has (past participle-suffer) from insomnia because he is nervous about his driving exam.

23. After relaxation therapy, he (past-slide) easily into a deep slumber.

24. Jean has (past participle-took) non-prescription pills to help her sleep.

25. Her doctor (past-tell) her not to do this.

26. She (past-disobey) his instruction.

27. Scientists have (past participle-describe) a deep stage of sleep as the rapid-eye-movement stage.

28. Freud (past-believe) our dreams reflect our unconscious wishes and fears.

or have plus past tense

have Looked

29. Many people have (past participle-dream) they could fly.

30. Dreamers have (past participle-dive) from cliffs without injuring themselves.

For the following sentences, change the verb to the indicated tenses in numbers 31-41.

Spies plant false information to mislead their pursuers.

31. past

32. future

33. present perfect

34. past perfect

35. future perfect

36. present progressive

37. past progressive

38. future progressive

39. present perfect progressive

40. past perfect progressive

41. future perfect progressive

For the following sentences, change the verb to the indicated tenses in numbers 42-50.

Luis writes in his journal every night.

42. past

43. future

44. present perfect

45. past perfect

46. future perfect

47. past progressive

48. future progressive

49. past perfect progressive

50. future perfect progressive

The following passage contains confusing shifts in verb tense. Identify the verbs. Then rewrite the passage so that the verbs are consistent and logical.

51-60.   Jackie Robinson, the first black American to play major league baseball, began his sports career at Pasadena City College. Then he transfers to the University of California at Los Angeles, where he was starring in football and track as well as baseball. After graduating, he joined the Kansas City Monarchs of the Negro Baseball League. While he plays there, he will be signed by Branch Rickey of the Brooklyn Dodgers. He plays for the Dodgers' Montreal farm team in 1946. In 1947, he became part of the Brooklyn Dodgers. He is named Rookie of the Year in 1947 and the National League's Most Valuable Player in 1949. To this day, fans of the Dodgers remembered him vividly.

4.3   Number and Person of Verbs

A verb that refers to one person or thing or quality takes the singular form; a verb that refers to more than one person, thing, or quality takes the plural.

Verbs used with first-person pronouns (I, we) are in the first person; verbs used with second-person pronouns (you, singular and plural) are in the second person. Verbs used with nouns or with third-person pronouns (it, he, she, they) are in the third person.

Verbs must agree with their subject in number. Singular subjects require singular verbs; plural subjects require plural verbs. Ignore descriptive words and phrases between the subject and verb when deciding if the verb should be singular or plural. Compound subjects require plural verbs. When the verb follows the subject in sentences beginning with *there*, *here* or *where*, be sure the verb agrees with the subject.

Example:

> Here are the names of the groups that will appear at the concert.

Names is the subject of the verb *are*. When a sentence uses a linking verb, the verb agrees with the subject, not the subject complement.

Example:

> The appearance of Ice Dog Rap was a surprise and a success.

Appearance is the singular subject. *A surprise and a success*, a plural construction, is the subject complement. Remember that indefinite pronouns such as *each* and *everyone* are always singular. Collective nouns usually take singular verbs unless the writer wishes to draw attention to the individual members of the group.

Identify the verb and its number and person in the following sentences.

61. Indira bought two new CDs.

62. Discalced and Defrocked, a rock band, plays loud music.

63. We enjoy their music.

64. You will like it too.

65. I want to buy tickets to their next concert.

66. Those tickets are expensive.

67. You may not be able to get good seats.

68. Fans of the Grateful Dead are called Deadheads.

69. Jerry Garcia, the group's leader, died in August, 1995.

70. Not everyone likes Cherry Garcia ice cream.

Correct the subject-verb agreement errors in the following sentences.

71. Although allergies caused by pollen is not a serious health problem, they can make one feel miserable.

72. School spirit and pride was very high.

73. The choice of tools for painting are as important as the type of paint.

74. Everyone know what it's like to be stuck in traffic.

75. There has been many times when an accident caused a traffic jam.

76. They are the drivers who is causing the problem.

77. Although fast food are cheap and convenient, it may be high in fat.

78. The worst thing about fast food are all the fried items.

79. A salad or a baked potato without butter are a healthful choice for lunch

80. The stereotype of women as weak and emotional have largely disappeared.

81. Another stereotype heard frequently were about the jolliness and kindness of the overweight.

82. There are no excuse for stereotypes, even if they are positive.

83. A shopping mall, with all its activities, provide a good place to hang out.

84. The style of the two rap groups are different.

85. Here is samples of different colors in which this pattern is available.

86. Each of the patterns match with a solid colored fabric.

87. Our football team win more often than it loses.

88. The quarterback, the tight end, and the punter has had a good season.

89. "Block that kick!" scream the crowd.

90. This group of sportscars are built for high performance at an economy price.

4.4 Voice

When a verb is in the active voice, somebody or something does something or acts. The subject of the verb acts or is. In the sentence "Nick loves his daughter Mona," Nick is acting. When a verb is in the passive voice, something is done to someone or something; the subject of the verb is acted upon. In the sentence "Mona is loved by her father, Nick," *Mona* is the subject of the sentence, and she is acted upon—she *is loved*—but she does not act.

In the following sentences, change active verbs to passive verbs, and change passive verbs to active verbs. You may also need to change other words in the sentence.

91. Nick wraps a package for his daughter's birthday present.

92. First he cuts a sheet of paper large enough to hold the box.

93. The paper was folded across the center of the box.

94. At each end, he folds the edges into triangles that meet.

95. The joined triangles were taped to the box's center

96. Then Nick tied a ribbon around the box.

97. A large green bow is attached to the ribbon.

98. Colorful butterflies are printed on the paper.

99. A plastic bumblebee nestles in the middle of the bow.

100. The present is given to his daughter when she wakes up on the morning of her birthday.

4.5 Moods

Verbs in the indicative mood express assertions or ask questions.

Examples:

I smile at the camera. Am I smiling?

Verbs in the imperative mood express request and commands. They are always in the second person.

Example:

Smile and say "cheese."

Verbs in the subjunctive mood express conditions contrary to fact, such as wishes, suggestions, or requests. The present subjunctive uses the base form of the verb. The past subjunctive of *be* is always *were.*

Examples:

If you were smiling, I would snap the picture. He asks that you smile and say "cheese."

In the following sentences, choose the correct form of the verb in parentheses.

101. If Ahmad (was/were) eighteen years old, he could register to vote.

102. The management asks that you (are/be) dressed properly to be admitted to the Swank Cafe.

103. Helen wishes that she (had/have) curly hair.

104. Sal recommends that Helen (try/tries) a loose permanent wave.

105. If Hideo (was/were) loved by Anita, she would marry him.

106. Claire's mother insists that dishes (are/be) washed as soon as dinner is over.

107. Roger moved that the meeting (be/is) adjourned.

108. The conductor requested that the tenor (sing/sings) more softly.

109. Professor Ohara asks that you (are/be) prepared to read the material aloud.

110. You wouldn't touch the iron if it (was/were) still hot.

 # Check Yourself

1. is running: transitive—*game* is the object (**Transitive and intransitive verbs**)

2. is running: intransitive (**Transitive and intransitive verbs**)

3. careen: intransitive (**Transitive and intransitive verbs**)

4. encourages: transitive—*customers* is the object (**Transitive and intransitive verbs**)

5. eat: transitive—*hot dogs, corn, and cotton candy* is the object (**Transitive and intransitive verbs**)

6. walk: intransitive (**Transitive and intransitive verbs**)

7. win: transitive—*ribbons* is the object (**Transitive and intransitive verbs**)

8. begin: transitive—*wilting* is the object (**Transitive and intransitive verbs**)

9. retired: intransitive (**Transitive and intransitive verbs**)

10. retired: transitive—*trophy* is the object (**Transitive and intransitive verbs**)

11. feels: linking (**Types of verbs**)

12. has applied: auxiliary (**Types of verbs**)

13. is located: auxiliary (**Types of verbs**)

14. is: linking (**Types of verbs**)

15. may refer: auxiliary (**Types of verbs**)

16. can be glazed: auxiliary (**Types of verbs**)

17. are: linking (**Types of verbs**)

18. must take: auxiliary (**Types of verbs**)

19. was: linking (**Types of verbs**)

20. will earn: auxiliary (**Types of verbs**)

21. slept (**Verb tenses**)

22. suffered (**Verb tenses**)

23. slid (**Verb tenses**)

24. taken (**Verb tenses**)

25. told (**Verb tenses**)

26. disobeyed (**Verb tenses**)

27. described (**Verb tenses**)

28. believed (**Verb tenses**)

29. dreamed (**Verb tenses**)

30. dived (**Verb tenses**)

31. planted (**Verb tenses**)

32. will plant (**Verb tenses**)

33. have planted (**Verb tenses**)

34. had planted (**Verb tenses**)

35. will have planted (**Verb tenses**)

36. are planting (**Verb tenses**)

37. were planting (**Verb tenses**)

38. will be planting (**Verb tenses**)

39. have been planting (**Verb tenses**)

40. had been planting (**Verb tenses**)

41. will have been planting (**Verb tenses**)

42. wrote (**Verb tenses**)

43. will write (**Verb tenses**)

44. has written (**Verb tenses**)

45. had written (**Verb tenses**)

46. will have written (**Verb tenses**)

47. was writing (**Verb tenses**)

48. will be writing (**Verb tenses**)

49. had been writing (**Verb tenses**)

50. will have been writing (**Verb tenses**)

51-60.

Jackie Robinson, the first black American to play major league baseball, began his sports career at Pasadena City College. Then he transferred to the University of California at Los Angeles, where he starred in football and track as well as baseball. After graduating, he joined the Kansas City Monarchs of the Negro Baseball League. While playing there, he was signed by Branch Rickey of the Brooklyn Dodgers. He played for the Brooklyn Dodgers' Montreal farm team in 1946. In 1947, he became part of the Brooklyn Dodgers. He was Rookie of the Year in 1947 and the National League's Most Valuable Player in 1949. To this day, fans of the Dodgers remember him vividly. **(Verb tenses)**

61. bought: third person singular **(Number and person of verbs)**

62. plays: third person singular (*A rock band* indicates the group is to be considered as a whole; thus it is singular.) **(Number and person of verbs)**

63. enjoy: first person plural **(Number and person of verbs)**

64. will like: second person; could be singular or plural **(Number and person of verbs)**

65. want: first person singular **(Number and person of verbs)**

66. are: third person plural **(Number and person of verbs)**

67. may be able: second person; could be singular or plural **(Number and person of verbs)**

68. are called: third person plural **(Number and person of verbs)**

69. died: third person singular **(Number and person of verbs)**

70. likes: third person singular (*Everyone* is an indefinite pronoun that is singular.) **(Number and person of verbs)**

71. Although allergies caused by pollen are not a serious problem, they can make one feel miserable. **(Subject- verb agreement)**

72. School spirit and pride were very high. **(Subject-verb agreement)**

73. The choice of tools for painting is as important as the type of paint. **(Subject-verb agreement)**

74. Everyone knows what it's like to be stuck in traffic. **(Subject-verb agreement)**

75. There have been many times when an accident caused a traffic jam. **(Subject-verb agreement)**

76. They are the drivers who are causing the problem. **(Subject-verb agreement)**

77. Although fast food is cheap and convenient, it may be high in fat. **(Subject-verb agreement)**

78. The worst thing about fast food is all the fried items. **(Subject-verb agreement)**

79. A salad or a baked potato without butter is a healthful choice for lunch. **(Subject-verb agreement)**

80. The stereotype of women as weak and emotional has largely disappeared. **(Subject-verb agreement)**

81. Another stereotype heard frequently was about the jolliness and kindness of the overweight. **(Subject-verb agreement)**

82. There is no excuse for stereotypes, even if they are positive. **(Subject-verb agreement)**

83. A shopping mall, with all its activities, provides a good place to hang out. **(Subject-verb agreement)**

84. The style of the two rap music groups is very different. **(Subject-verb agreement)**

85. Here are samples of different colors in which this pattern is available. **(Subject-verb agreement)**

86. Each of the patterns matches with a solid coordinating fabric. **(Subject-verb agreement)**

87. Our football team wins more often than it loses. **(Subject-verb agreement)**

88. The quarterback, the tight end, and the punter have had a good season. **(Subject-verb agreement)**

89. "Block that kick!" screams the crowd. **(Subject-verb agreement)**

90. This group of sportscars is built for high performance at an economy price. **(Subject-verb agreement)**

91. A package is wrapped by Nick for his daughter's birthday present. **(Voice)**

92. A sheet of paper large enough to hold the box is first cut by him. **(Voice)**

93. He folded the paper across the center of the box. **(Voice)**

94. The edges at each end are folded into triangles that meet. **(Voice)**

95. He tapes the joined triangles to the box's center. **(Voice)**

96. A ribbon is tied around the box by Nick. **(Voice)**

97. He attaches a huge green bow to the ribbon. **(Voice)**

98. The paper has colorful butterflies printed on it. **(Voice)**

99. A plastic bumblebee is nestled in the middle of the bow. **(Voice)**

100. He gives the present to his daughter when she wakes up on the morning of her birthday. **(Voice)**

101. were **(Mood)**

102. be **(Mood)**

103. had **(Mood)**

104. try **(Mood)**

105. were **(Mood)**

106. be **(Mood)**

107. be **(Mood)**

108. sing **(Mood)**

109. be **(Mood)**

110. were **(Mood)**

Grade Yourself

Circle the numbers of the questions you missed, then fill in the total incorrect for each topic. If you answered more than three questions incorrectly, you need to focus on that topic. (If a topic has less than three questions and you had at least one wrong, we suggest you study that topic also. Read your textbook, a review book, or ask your teacher for help.)

Subject: Verbs

Topic	Question Numbers	Number Incorrect
Transitive and intransitive verbs	1, 2, 3, 4, 5, 6, 7, 8, 9, 10	
Types of verbs	11, 12, 13, 14, 15, 16, 17, 18, 19, 20	
Verb tenses	21, 22, 23, 24, 25, 26, 27, 28, 29, 30, 31, 32, 33, 34, 35, 36, 37, 38, 39, 40, 41, 42, 43, 44, 45, 46, 47, 48, 49, 50, 51, 52, 53, 54, 55, 56, 57, 58, 59, 60	
Number and person of verbs	61, 62, 63, 64, 65, 66, 67, 68, 69, 70	
Subject-verb agreement	71, 72, 73, 74, 75, 76, 77, 78, 79, 80, 81, 82, 83, 84, 85, 86, 87, 88, 89, 90	
Voice	91, 92, 93, 94, 95, 96, 97, 98, 99, 100	
Mood	101, 102, 103, 104, 105, 106, 107, 108, 109, 110	

Verbals

5

 Test Yourself

5.1 Infinitives

Although *to* is usually a preposition, when it appears before the basic form of a verb, the verb is the infinitive form. An infinitive and its subject, subject complement, or modifiers form an infinitive phrase.

Infinitives and infinitive phrases can be used as nouns, adjectives, or adverbs.

Examples:

To choose nutritious foods requires reading package labels.

To choose nutritious foods is an infinitive phrase used as a noun because it is the subject of the sentence.

The best time to shop is in the morning.

To shop is an infinitive used as an adjective modifying *time*.

Compare prices carefully to avoid overpaying.

To avoid overpaying is an infinitive phrase used as an adverb modifying *compare*.

In the following sentences, identify whether the infinitives or infinitive phrases are used as nouns, adjectives, or adverbs.

1. Computer-aided drafting is useful to improve accuracy, legibility, and consistency.

2. The are many useful texts to read on the subject.

3. To understand the texts, however, working at a computer while reading may be necessary.

4. To draw a model precisely becomes simple when you know how to use the system.

5. Some of the basic drawing commands are to line, to point, to circle and to zoom.

6. The instructor wanted to ensure the students knew the basic commands before he introduced more complicated commands.

7. To do this, he had them draw simple geometric diagrams.

8. Later in the course, the students learned to draw architectural plans.

9. Design changes in engineering drawing are easier to make on the computer.

10. To design stage sets is another use for computerized drafting.

Do not place words between *to* and the basic form of a verb unless splitting the infinitive makes the sentence less confusing.

Example:

"Splitting an infinitive may make a sentence difficult to easily read" should be changed to "Splitting an infinitive may make a sentence difficult to read easily."

However, in the sentence "Chris needs to more than understand his problems; he also need to cope with them," placing *more than* elsewhere in the sentence

42

would make it harder to grasp the contrast that is the sentence's essential meaning.

Rewrite any sentences in which the infinitive should not be split.

11. "To seek out new civilizations, to boldly go when no one has gone before: These are the voyages of the starship *Enterprise*."

12. The announcer wants the audience to clearly see the scope of the starship's travels.

13. When Tomas saw the tamales, he wanted to immediately eat them.

14. Romeo wanted to more than love Juliet; he wanted to marry her.

15. Women have the right to not be harassed in the workplace.

16. After vigorous exercise, it's a good idea to slowly drink several glasses of water.

17. To perfectly make pie crust, blend the flour and shortening until they resemble coarse meal.

18. As the drought grew longer, the tribe continued to fervently pray for rain.

19. Marie was warned to with great care consider the consequence of her daring actions.

20. The lioness began to ferociously devour her prey.

5.2 Participles

The present participle and the past participle of a verb function as adjectives.

Participial phrases consist of participles and the words that modify them.

An absolute phrase modifies the entire sentence. Because sentences with absolute phrases may sound awkward, some writers prefer to change the absolute phrase to a subordinate clause.

Example:

"The World Series having begun, the ratings of the network that broadcast it increased" could be changed to "Because the World Series had begun, the rating of the network that broadcast it increased."

Place participial phrases as close as possible to the words they modify. Failure to do so may produce confusion.

Example:

Leah thought she saw a ghost riding a bicycle without a head.

Obviously, no bicycle has a head. The sentence should read "Leah thought she saw a ghost without a head riding a bicycle."

Be sure there is a word in the sentence, the participial phrase can logically modify. When there is no such word, the participial phrase is called a dangling participle.

Example:

Basking in the sunshine at the beach, my tan grew darker.

Basking in the sunshine at the beach cannot logically modify *tan*. A revised sentence might read:

Basking in the sunshine at the beach, I noticed my tan growing darker.

Underline the participle or participial phrase in each of the following sentences.

21. Haunted by ghosts, Ebenezer Scrooge changes his life.

22. Edna Pontellier, protagonist of *The Awakening*, becoming aware of her talent, takes up painting.

23. Concerned, Walt Whitman helped nurse wounded Civil War soldiers.

24. Henry James and T. S. Eliot, born in the United States, spent most of their lives in England.

25. In *The Sun Also Rises*, Jake Barnes, wounded physically and mentally, reacts stoically.

26. In *The Color Purple*, Celie, tormented by her husband, writes letters to God.

27. Sammy in the story "A & P," being innocent, does not realize the consequences of his action.

28. Pinocchio, changing his form, becomes a real boy.

29. Rolling down the hill, Jack and Jill were injured.

30. In the story "Where Are You Going, Where Have You Been," Arnold Friend's making insinuating remarks frightens Connie.

Change the absolute phrases in the following sentences to subordinate clauses.

31. Needing to make the putt to win the tournament, Lee Trevino lined it up carefully.

32. Weakened by the attack on her, Monica Seles retired from tennis for two years.

33. Baseball season having ended, the players returned to their home.

34. Being temperatures are often hot in September, football players sweat while practicing.

35. Having much hot weather, Houston logically chose a domed stadium so it could be air conditioned.

36. Trying to avoid injury, gymnasts warm up gradually before a meet.

37. Watching the close game, the crowd roared with excitement.

38. Frightened by reports of crowd violence, some soccer fans chose not to attend the match.

39. Upset by the umpire's decision, the crowd booed.

40. The goalie having misjudged the shot, the opposing team scored.

Rewrite any sentences in which the participial phrase is misplaced.

41. Needing a tuneup, my father took his car to the garage.

42. The realtor sold the house to a family having leaky plumbing.

43. Having lived there for many years, the Jeffersons ignored the problem.

44. Bought at an auction, Joan gave the antique sword to her son.

45. The suspect was described as being five feet tall, and having brown eyes weighing 120 pounds.

46. Running from the bank, the suspect tripped over a crack in the sidewalk.

47. Pickled or raw, I don't like cucumbers.

48. Hanging on the line, I saw the clothes.

49. Carried away by grief, tears ran down Keenan's cheeks.

50. Prodded by the buzzing alarm, Winona jumped out of bed.

Rewrite the following sentences to correct the dangling participles.

51. Working in a factory, the microwave oven make lunch hour more enjoyable.

52. We glanced at the menu waiting for the waiter to arrive.

53. Having decided, the waiter took our order.

54. Without waiting long, our dinner appeared.

55. The bank quickly foreclosed, being unable to make payments on the property.

56. Watching a classic film, advertisements that interrupt are especially annoying.

57. The attendant washed my windshield waiting in line for gas.

58. Entered in a public speaking contest at the age of twelve, Kareem's mother was proud of him.

59. News item: "Diving into dishwashers, prowling around the pool, prying in pantries, California homeowners report a plague of mice."

60. Playing in 2,131 consecutive baseball games, Ty Cobb's record was broken by Cal Ripken, Jr.

5.3 Gerunds

Gerunds are present participles of verbs. They function as nouns in sentences.

Example:

Stealing trash from recycling containers is illegal in many cities.

Stealing trash is a gerund that is the subject of the verb *is*, so it functions as a noun.

When a noun or pronoun precedes a gerund, the noun or pronoun should be in the possessive case.

Example:

Many cities do not permit your [not "you"] stealing recyclable materials.

Stealing recyclable materials is a gerund phrase functioning as the object of the verb; since it is a gerund, the pronoun must be possessive.

Identify the gerund or gerund phrase in each sentence and state if it is used as a subject, subject complement, object of a verb, or object of a preposition.

61. Recycling trash has become profitable as well as environmentally sound.

62. In some states, it is the law that consumers be paid for returning aluminum beverage cans.

63. Cities provide residents with different containers for recycling each kind of trash.

64. In other cities, laws prohibit scavenging from recycling containers.

65. One way to help prevent energy depletion is walking instead of driving.

66. Bundling up newspapers to take them to a recycling center can save space in landfills.

67. Trash in landfills, covered with dirt and not exposed to air, is prevented from biodegrading.

68. Methane gas, produced as a byproduct of cattle's digestion, is breaking down the ozone layer.

69. To wear a cloth mask in dirty air prevents wheezing and choking.

70. The roar of traffic, the blaring of radios, the shouting of children: All these are good for causing a headache.

Some of the following sentences use a noun or pronoun correctly with a gerund; some do not. If the noun or pronoun is not in the correct form, write the correct form.

71. Carmen doesn't like Peter driving so fast.

72. In some states your going to a traffic school can substitute for paying a fine if you get a traffic ticket.

73. Ruben's off-key singing hurt John's ears.

74. Elizabeth enjoyed Sandra joking.

75. Derek and Yvonne knew that their refusing to answer personal questions made them look unfriendly.

76. Their friends frequent and intrusive questioning made them uncomfortable.

77. You behaving in a shy manner was misinterpreted.

78. The possibility of his withholding information exists.

79. The dog constant barking woke up the whole neighborhood.

80. Because of her hurrying to prepare dinner, Jasmine burned the potatoes.

5.4 Maintaining Parallelism of Verbals

When using verbals in a sentence, be sure they are grammatically parallel. When using more than two verbals with *to* or *for*, either use *to* or *for* for the first verbal and not the others, or use it for all the verbals. Do not use *to* or *for* with some but not all of the verbals.

Correct any errors in parallelism of verbals in the following sentences.

81. Humor can be used to wound as well as to amuse.

82. Ethnic jokes are embarrassing, degrading, and lower self-esteem.

83. Recycled water is used for irrigating parks and golf courses, washing streets and sidewalks, and to flush toilets.

84. It is usually not safe for drinking, cooking, or for bathing.

85. To die, to sleep, and dreaming: Hamlet mentions these in his soliloquy.

86. Stress is put on the back's muscles when one stoops, lifts, or if you suddenly twist.

87. Observing closely and taking accurate notes are necessary for doing field observation.

88. Daydreams of instant success include winning a lottery, becoming a movie star, and to find buried treasure.

89. The Hebrew word *Shalom* is used to mean peace and to greet people.

90. Young children like to sing, to play, and coloring.

Check Yourself

1. to improve accuracy, legibility, and consistency: adverb—modifies *is useful* (**Infinitives**)

2. to read on the subject: adjective—modifies *texts* (**Infinitives**)

3. To understand the texts: adverb—modifies *may be necessary* (**Infinitives**)

4. to draw a model precisely: noun—subject of verb *becomes* (**Infinitives**)

5. to line, to point, to circle, and to zoom: noun—subject complement (**Infinitives**)

6. to ensure the students knew the basic commands: noun—object of verb *wanted* (**Infinitives**)

7. to do this: adverb—modifies *in order* (**Infinitives**)

8. to draw architectural plans: noun—object of verb *learned* (**Infinitives**)

9. to make on the computer: adverb—modifies *are easier* (**Infinitives**)

10. To design stage sets: noun—subject of verb *is* (**Infinitives**)

11. "To seek out new civilizations, to go boldly where no one has gone before: these are the voyages of the starship *Enterprise*." (**Split infinitives**)

12. The announcer wants us to see clearly the scope of the starship's travels. (**Split infinitives**)

13. When Tomas saw the tamales, he wanted to eat them immediately. (**Split infinitives**)

14. correct; rewriting the sentence would make it awkward. (**Split infinitives**)

15. Women have the right not to be harassed in the workplace. (**Split infinitives**)

16. After vigorous exercise, it's a good idea to drink several glasses of water slowly. (**Split infinitives**)

17. To make pie crust perfectly, blend the flour and shortening until they resemble coarse meal. (**Split infinitives**)

18. As the drought grew longer, the tribe continued to pray fervently for rain. (**Split infinitives**)

19. Marie was warned to consider with great care the consequences of her daring actions. (**Split infinitives**)

20. The lioness began ferociously to devour her prey. (**Split infinitives**)

21. Haunted by ghosts (**Identifying participles and participial phrases**)

22. becoming aware of her talents (**Identifying participles and participial phrases**)

23. Concerned (**Identifying participles and participial phrases**)

24. born in the United States (**Identifying participles and participial phrases**)

25. wounded physically and mentally (**Identifying participles and participial phrases**)

26. tormented by her husband (**Identifying participles and participial phrases**)

27. being innocent (**Identifying participles and participial phrases**)

28. changing his form (**Identifying participles and participial phrases**)

29. Rolling down the hill (**Identifying participles and participial phrases**)

30. making insinuating remarks (**Identifying participles and participial phrases**)

31. Because he needed to make the putt to win the tournament, Lee Trevino lined it up carefully. (**Absolute phrases**)

32. Because she was weakened by the attack on her, Monica Seles retired from tennis for two years. (**Absolute phrases**)

33. When baseball season ended, the players returned to their home. (**Absolute phrases**)

34. Because temperatures are often hot in September, football players sweat while practicing. (**Absolute phrases**)

35. Because it has much hot weather, Houston logically chose a domed stadium so that it could be air conditioned. (**Absolute phrases**)

36. Gymnasts warm up gradually before a meet, trying to avoid injury. (**Absolute phrases**)

37. The crowd roared with excitement while watching the close game. (**Absolute phrases**)

38. Because they were frightened by reports of crowd violence, some soccer fans chose not to attend the match. (**Absolute phrases**)

39. When the umpire made a faulty decision, the crowd booed. (**Absolute phrases**)

40. Because the goalie misjudged the shot, the opposing team scored. (**Absolute phrases**)

41. Because his car needed a tuneup, my father took it to the garage. (**Misplaced participles**)

42. The realtor sold the house that had leaky plumbing to a family. (**Misplaced participles**)

43. correct (**Misplaced participles**)

44. Joan gave her son the antique sword she bought at an auction. (**Misplaced participles**)

45. The suspect was described as being five feet tall, weighing 120 pounds, and having brown eyes. (**Misplaced participles**)

46. correct (**Misplaced participles**)

47. I don't like pickled or raw cucumbers. (**Misplaced participles**)

48. I saw the clothes hanging on the line. (**Misplaced participles**)

49. Keenan was carried away by grief, and tears ran down his cheeks. (**Misplaced participles**)

50. correct (**Misplaced participles**)

51. When I worked in a factory, the microwave oven made lunch hour more enjoyable. (**Dangling participles**)

52. We glanced at the menu while we waited for the waiter to arrive. **(Dangling participles)**

53. After we decided what we wanted, the waiter took our order. **(Dangling participles)**

54. We didn't wait long before our dinner appeared. **(Dangling participles)**

55. The bank quickly foreclosed when the owner was unable to make payments on the property. **(Dangling participles)**

56. When one watches a classic film, advertisements that interrupt are especially annoying. **(Dangling participles)**

57. The attendant washed my windshield while I was waiting in line for gas. **(Dangling participles)**

58. Entered in a public speaking contest at the age of twelve, Kareem made his mother proud of him. **(Dangling participles)**

59. News item: "California homeowners report a plague of mice diving into dishwashers, prowling around the pool, and prying in pantries. **(Dangling participles)**

60. Cal Ripken, playing in 2,131 consecutive baseball games, broke Ty Cobb's record. **(Dangling participles)**

61. Recycling trash: subject **(Gerunds)**

62. returning aluminum beverage cans: object of preposition **(Gerunds)**

63. recycling each kind of trash: object of preposition **(Gerunds)**

64. scavenging from recycling containers: object of verb **(Gerunds)**

65. walking instead of driving: subject complement **(Gerunds)**

66. Bundling up newspapers: subject **(Gerunds)**

67. biodegrading: object of preposition **(Gerunds)**

68. breaking down the ozone layer: subject complement **(Gerunds)**

69. wheezing and choking: object **(Gerunds)**

70. causing a headache: object of preposition **(Gerunds)**

71. Peter's **(Using possessives with gerunds)**

72. correct **(Using possessives with gerunds)**

73. correct **(Using possessives with gerunds)**

74. Sandra's **(Using possessives with gerunds)**

75. correct **(Using possessives with gerunds)**

76. friends' **(Using possessives with gerunds)**

77. Your **(Using possessives with gerunds)**

78. correct **(Using possessives with gerunds)**

79. dog's **(Using possessives with gerunds)**

80. correct **(Using possessives with gerunds)**

81. correct **(Parallelism of verbals)**

82. Ethnic jokes embarrass, degrade, and lower self-esteem. **(Parallelism of verbals)**

83. Recycled water is used for irrigating parks and golf courses, washing streets and sidewalks, and flushing toilets. **(Parallelism of verbals)**

84. It is usually not safe for drinking, for cooking, or for bathing. **(Parallelism of verbals)**

85. To die, to sleep, and to dream: Hamlet mentions these in his soliloquy. **(Parallelism of verbals)**

86. Stress is put on the back's muscles when one stoops, lifts, or twists suddenly. **(Parallelism of verbals)**

87. correct **(Parallelism of verbals)**

88. Daydreams of instant success include winning a lottery, becoming a movie star, and finding buried treasure. **(Parallelism of verbals)**

89. correct **(Parallelism of verbals)**

90. Children like to sing, to play, and to color. **(Parallelism of verbals)**

Grade Yourself

Circle the numbers of the questions you missed, then fill in the total incorrect for each topic. If you answered more than three questions incorrectly, you need to focus on that topic. (If a topic has less than three questions and you had at least one wrong, we suggest you study that topic also. Read your textbook, a review book, or ask your teacher for help.)

Subject: Verbals

Topic	Question Numbers	Number Incorrect
Infinitives	1, 2, 3, 4, 5, 6, 7, 8, 9, 10	
Split infinitives	11, 12, 13, 14, 15, 16, 17, 18, 19, 20	
Identifying participles and participial phrases	21, 22, 23, 24, 25, 26, 27, 28, 29, 30	
Absolute phrases	31, 32, 33, 34, 35, 36, 37, 38, 39, 40	
Misplaced participles	41, 42, 43, 44, 45, 46, 47, 48, 49, 50	
Dangling participles	51, 52, 53, 54, 55, 56, 57, 58, 59, 60	
Gerunds	61, 62, 63, 64, 65, 66, 67, 68, 69, 70	
Using possessives with gerunds	71, 72, 73, 74, 75, 76, 77, 78, 79, 80	
Parallelism of verbals	81, 82, 83, 84, 85, 86, 87, 88, 89, 90	

Adjectives and Adverbs

6

 Test Yourself

6.1 Types of Adjectives

When two adjectives in a row describe the same word, and the order of the adjectives does not affect meaning, the adjectives are *coordinate*. Use commas to separate coordinate adjectives.

Proper adjectives must have an initial capital letter.

Examples:

Baroque music, Gothic cathedrals, Spanish art

Hyphenate *compound adjectives*.

Example:

part-time instructor

Spell out numbers that begin a sentence or that do not require more than two words to spell out.

Identify the type of adjective in the sentences below, and indicate if it is used correctly by writing C for correct, and N for incorrect.

1. Owning a restaurant is a full-time occupation.

2. Elena Rodriguez owns El Rancho, which serves Mexican food.

3. She has 3 cooks working in the kitchen.

4. When the restaurant opened, the new hired servers were inexperienced.

5. Consequently, slow, sloppy service sometimes caused problems.

6. Two patrons complained to Ms. Rodriguez during the first week the restaurant was open.

7. One of the best dishes is chicken Yucatan style.

8. It has a pungent, hot flavor.

9. With the passage of time, the restaurant has become a better-managed place.

10. On Saturday, the restaurant served 100 dinners.

6.2 Use of Adjectives in Sentences

Adjectives usually precede the nouns they modify.

Predicate adjectives follow linking verbs and describe the subject of the verb.

Insert the adjective in parentheses in the correct place in the following sentences.

11. (disgusted) When I saw the alien in the science fiction movie, I became.

12. (hostile) Not all aliens in science fiction films are.

13. (struggling) Some come from advanced civilizations with the intent of helping humanity.

14. (grotesque) The face of Frankenstein frightened the villagers.

15. (cowardly) The lion in *The Wizard of Oz* appears.

16. (nauseated) I became after eating all of the giant-size popcorn.

17. (gory) People may become numb after seeing too many scenes.

18. (contorted) In the photo, the victim's face expressed his fear.

19. (brutal) The creature horrified the children who were watching the film.

20. (dispassionate) To render a just verdict, jurors must be.

6.3 Adverbs

Adverbs modify verbs, adjectives, other adverbs, verbals, prepositional phrases, and sentences.

Place adverbs close to the word or words they modify.

If the adverb in the following sentences is placed so that the sentence's meaning is clear, write C. If the sentence is confusing or unclear, write U.

21. A book I read carefully explained how to grow roses.

22. Ferns are the only green plants that I grow indoors.

23. Growing vegetables organically is not difficult.

24. I waited hopefully for the tomatoes to ripen.

25. Hopefully, the tomatoes will ripen soon.

26. Always easy to grow, radishes are fun for children to plant.

27. The corn I picked quickly was eaten at the picnic.

28. A trellis for growing cucumbers should be very tall and sturdy.

29. Snails are a pest that gardeners usually worry about.

30. It is quite apparent that a home vegetable garden saves money.

6.4 Negatives

Negative words may function as adjectives, adverbs, or nouns.

Although double negatives are usually unacceptable, two negatives may be used to produce a positive meaning. However, some grammarians and rhetoricians disapprove of this construction.

Example:

The critic wrote that although the book's subject matter was ordinary, the writer's approach to it was not uninteresting.

If the negative word in the following sentences is an adjective, write AJ. If it is an adverb, write AV. If it is a noun, write N.

31. Elaine never forgets to fasten her seatbelt.

32. Some states have no laws requiring bicycle helmets.

33. None of the motorcyclists wore shorts.

34. Congresswoman Chavez voted "no" on the resolution.

35. Congressman Samuels was not present for the vote.

36. It is better to be late than never to arrive for an appointment.

37. Nothing can be done about the problem.

38. The city's budget for library services is not large.

39. In some cultures, nodding the head is a gesture meaning "no.

40. The jury declared the defendant was not guilty.

If the sentence or phrase uses negatives correctly, write C. If it does not use them correctly, write N.

41. "I don't get no respect," says Rodney Dangerfield.

42. Unlike Rodney Dangerfield, Serena George don't use no double negatives.

43. "I Can't Get No Satisfaction"

44. It's hardly necessary to criticize grammar in song lyrics.

45. In the past, there were scarcely any female standup comics.

46. People can't scarcely stop laughing when they watch *Roseanne*.

47. Lucy and Desi didn't have no children when the *I Love Lucy* was first broadcast.

48. I won't never forget the show when Lucy worked in a candy factory.

49. It's not uncommon for comedians to laugh at their own jokes.

50. Paul won't let nobody tell his jokes but me.

6.5 Choosing Adjectives or Adverbs

Use adjectives to modify nouns and pronouns and as predicate adjectives.

Use adverbs to modify verbs, adjectives, other adverbs, verbals, prepositional phrases, and sentences.

Identify the correct word in parentheses.

51. Some animals behave (different/differently) than humans when reacting to a stimulus.

52. Since humans and apes are similar mammals, they may behave (similar/similarly).

53. The cat cried (loud/loudly) when I accidentally stepped on her tail.

54. I felt (bad/badly) when I heard the cat howl.

55. But the cat was not hurt (bad/badly).

56. A moth brushed (soft/softly) against Carol's cheek.

57. It's (wrong/wrongly) to say bats get tangled in people's hair.

58. Most bats are (shy/shyly) creatures.

59. Bats eat (harmful/harmfully) insects.

60. The skin of a snake feels (dry/dryly) when you touch it.

61. The (deceptive/deceptively) slim neck of a giraffe is actually quite strong.

62. The sloth is a creature that moves very (slow/slowly).

63. Birds of prey such as hawks soar (high/highly) in the air.

64. The (extreme/extremely) rapid descent of falcons helps them to catch their prey.

65. The Discovery Channel presents (real/really) compelling nature programs.

66. Ian smells (good/well) when he puts on after shave lotion.

67. After her warm-up in exercise class, Dawn moved (well/good).

68. John Jefferson has arthritis so (bad/badly) that he can't touch his toes.

69. The football team was so (inept/ineptly) that the fans cheered when the franchise moved.

70. Martina plays a (good/well) game of tennis.

71. Ivan plays tennis (good/well).

72. Mario Andretti and Richard Petty were (real/really) good race car drivers.

73. When Ted drives too (quick/fast), he risks getting a speeding ticket.

74. At the four-way signal, Maria came to a (full/fully) stop.

75. Susan slammed on the brakes (hard/hardly) as the car next to her darted into her lane.

76. (Sure/surely) she did the right thing to prevent an accident.

77. A four-door sedan is a (practical/practically) car.

78. The (awkward/awkwardly) shaped fender of that car is unattractive.

79. Jeeps move very (agile/agilely) in all kinds of terrain.

80. Do men criticize women drivers because they are upset when women drive (aggressive/aggressively)?

6.6 Comparative and Superlative Forms of Adjectives and Adverbs

Regular adjectives and adverbs form the comparative by adding -er or more. They form the superlative by adding -est or most. Do not use both the -er form and the word more to form a comparative. Do not use both the -est form and the word most to form a superlative.

Some adjectives and adverbs—for example *bad, badly, good, little, many,* and *much*—have irregular comparatives and superlatives.

Use the comparative to compare two items; use the superlative to compare three or more items.

Adjectives that describe absolute concepts—such as *unique, complete,* and *dead*—cannot be used in the comparative or superlative.

In the following sentences, if comparative and superlative forms of adjectives and adverbs are used correctly, write C. If they are used incorrectly, write I.

81. Flyway Airlines serves the most tastiest food in the sky.

82. The instructor told the students that if they completed the assignments, they would not get a grade worst than C.

83. Although speeding and improper turns cause accidents, drunk driving is the most dangerous problem.

84. Paul's dog barks constantly and chases children; it's the baddest animal in the neighborhood.

85. Of the two rock groups, Rompo is the best.

86. When working on a jigsaw puzzle, it's easier to see a more clearer image as you progress.

87. Evan's twenty-first birthday was the most perfect day of his life.

88. Sunset over Lake Largo was the most beautiful sight I had ever seen.

89. The sky was streaked with the deepest shades of violet and rose.

90. Tiny Tim was the littlest child in the Cratchit family.

91. Marsha's new hat was the most unique piece of headgear that Barbara had ever seen.

92. As the party went on and people became more animated, the noise level grew.

93. Pretzels and potato chips were served, but popcorn was the most popular snack.

94. Warm soda is more fizzier than cold soda.

95. Of jellybeans, brownies, and ice cream, ice cream is the higher in fat.

In the following sentences, write the correct form of the adjective or adverb in parentheses. Use comparative or superlative as indicated at the end of the sentence.

96. Who is the (credible) of the two witnesses? [comparative]

97. When the students misunderstood the question, the teacher tried to explain it (clearly). [comparative]

98. This racing bike is (light) than that one. [comparative]

99. Toward the end of the race, the (less) experienced driver is likely to make a mistake. [superlative]

100. The driver who wins the pole position has the (fast) qualifying time. [superlative]

101. Michael Andretti is (old) than his cousin John. [comparative]

103. Which of the two is the (good) driver? [comparative]

103. Does either of them drive (well) than Al Unser, Jr.? [comparative]

104. Team America's cars often run (fast) than Team Champion's. [comparative[

105. Angela's team prepares (carefully) for every race. [superlative]

6.7 Choosing the Correct Conjunctive Adverb

Conjunctive adverbs signal logical relationships such as addition, comparison, contrast, time, or consequences.

Circle the conjunctive adverb that is the more logical in the sentences below.

106. Early humans only saw lights in the sky. (Later/Likewise) we learned some of these stars are planets.

107. Telescopes enriched our knowledge of the planets; (thus/subsequently) space probes and satellites provided more information.

108. Stars produce their own light and heat; planets do not. (Also/Besides) this difference, in the night sky, planets shine steadily.

109. (Conversely/Still)stars twinkle.

110. The surface temperature of the planets is related to their distance from the sun. (Consequently/ Still) Venus is quite hot, while Neptune is cold.

111. Instruments that detect infrared radiation and radio waves are used to measure the temperature of the planets; (however/furthermore), these instruments do not measure low temperatures easily.

112. (Finally/Therefore) estimates for the temperature of Pluto, the planet farthest from Earth, are not precise.

113. To determine if life as we know it exists in space, (still/first) we must determine if there is water on the planet.

114. (Similarly/Besides), if the life form resembles us, the planet's atmosphere must contain oxygen.

115. Earth and Mars have water vapor in their atmosphere; Venus's and Jupiter's atmospheres contain water vapor (also/surely).

116. (Certainly/Instead) the discovery of life forms in the universe would change our ideas about humanity.

 # Check Yourself

1. N: *full-time* is a compound adjective. (**Types of adjectives**)

2. C: *Mexican* is a proper adjective. (**Types of adjectives**)

3. N: *three* should be written out. (**Types of adjectives**)

4. C: *new hired* is not a coordinate adjective because changing the order of the words would change the meaning. (**Types of adjectives**)

5. C: *slow* and *sloppy* are coordinate adjectives. (**Types of adjectives**)

6. C: *two* (**Types of adjectives**)

7. N: *Yucatan* is a proper adjective. (**Types of adjectives**)

8. N: *pungent* and *hot* are coordinate adjectives. (**Types of adjectives**)

9. N: *better* and *managed* are compound adjectives. (**Types of adjectives**)

10. C: *100* (**Types of adjectives**)

11. became disgusted (**Use of adjectives in sentences**)

12. are hostile (**Use of adjectives in sentences**)

13. struggling humanity (**Use of adjectives in sentences**)

14. grotesque face (**Use of adjectives in sentences**)

15. appears cowardly (**Use of adjectives in sentences**)

16. became nauseated (**Use of adjectives in sentences**)

17. gory scenes (**Use of adjectives in sentences**)

18. contorted face (**Use of adjectives in sentences**)

19. brutal creature (**Use of adjectives in sentences**)

20. be dispassionate (**Use of adjectives in sentences**)

21. U: read carefully or explained carefully? (**Adverbs**)

22. C (**Adverbs**)

23. C (**Adverbs**)

24. C (**Adverbs**)

25. U: can tomatoes hope they ripen? (**Adverbs**)

26. C (**Adverbs**)

27. U: *picked quickly* or *quickly eaten* (**Adverbs**)

28. C (**Adverbs**)

29. C (**Adverbs**)

30. C (**Adverbs**)

31. AV: *never* modifies the verb *forgets.* (**Adverbs**)

32. AD: *no* modifies the noun *laws.* (**Adverbs**)

33. N: *None* is the subject of the verb *wore.* (**Adverbs**)

34. N: *no* is the object of the verb *voted.* (**Adverbs**)

35. AV: *not* modifies the adjective *present.* (**Adverbs**)

36. AJ: *never* modifies the infinitive *to arrive* which is used as a noun. (**Adverbs**)

37. N: *Nothing* is the subject of the verb *can be done.* (**Adverbs**)

38. AV: *not* modifies the adjective *large.* (**Adverbs**)

39. N: *no* is the object of the verb *meaning.* (**Adverbs**)

40. AV: *not* modifies the adjective *guilty.* (**Adverbs**)

41. N (**Negatives**)

42. N (**Negatives**)

43. N (**Negatives**)

44. C (**Negatives**)

45. C (**Negatives**)

46. N (**Negatives**)

47. N (**Negatives**)

48. N (**Negatives**)

49. C (**Negatives**)

50. N (**Negatives**)

51. differently (**Choosing adjectives or adverbs**)

52. similarly (**Choosing adjectives or adverbs**)

53. loudly (**Choosing adjectives or adverbs**)

54. *bad*: *Felt* is a linking verb that takes a predicate adjective. **(Choosing adjectives or adverbs)**

55. badly **(Choosing adjectives or adverbs)**

56. softly **(Choosing adjectives or adverbs)**

57. *wrong* modifies *is*, a verb requiring a predicate adjective. **(Choosing adjectives or adverbs)**

58. shy **(Choosing adjectives or adverbs)**

59. harmful **(Choosing adjectives or adverbs)**

60. dry **(Choosing adjectives or adverbs)**

61. deceptively **(Choosing adjectives or adverbs)**

62. slowly **(Choosing adjectives or adverbs)**

63. high: both the adjective and adverb form **(Choosing adjectives or adverbs)**

64. extremely **(Choosing adjectives or adverbs)**

65. really **(Choosing adjectives or adverbs)**

66. good: modifies *Ian*, not *smells* **(Choosing adjectives or adverbs)**

67. well **(Choosing adjectives or adverbs)**

68. bad: modifies *arthritis* **(Choosing adjectives or adverbs)**

69. inept **(Choosing adjectives or adverbs)**

70. good **(Choosing adjectives or adverbs)**

71. well **(Choosing adjectives or adverbs)**

72. really **(Choosing adjectives or adverbs)**

73. fast: both the adjective and adverb form **(Choosing adjectives or adverbs)**

74. full **(Choosing adjectives or adverbs)**

75. hard: both the adjective and adverb form **(Choosing adjectives or adverbs)**

76. *Surely*: modifies the whole sentence **(Choosing adjectives or adverbs)**

77. practical **(Choosing adjectives or adverbs)**

78. awkwardly **(Choosing adjectives or adverbs)**

79. agilely **(Choosing adjectives or adverbs)**

80. aggressively **(Choosing adjectives or adverbs)**

81. I **(Comparative and superlative forms of adjectives and adverbs)**

82. I **(Comparative and superlative forms of adjectives and adverbs)**

83. C (**Comparative and superlative forms of adjectives and adverbs**)

84. I (**Comparative and superlative forms of adjectives and adverbs**)

85. I (**Comparative and superlative forms of adjectives and adverbs**)

86. I (**Comparative and superlative forms of adjectives and adverbs**)

87. I (**Comparative and superlative forms of adjectives and adverbs**)

88. C (**Comparative and superlative forms of adjectives and adverbs**)

89. C (**Comparative and superlative forms of adjectives and adverbs**)

90. C (**Comparative and superlative forms of adjectives and adverbs**)

91. I (**Comparative and superlative forms of adjectives and adverbs**)

92. C (**Comparative and superlative forms of adjectives and adverbs**)

93. C (**Comparative and superlative forms of adjectives and adverbs**)

94. I (**Comparative and superlative forms of adjectives and adverbs**)

95. I (**Comparative and superlative forms of adjectives and adverbs**)

96. more credible (**Comparative and superlative forms of adjectives and adverbs**)

97. more clearly (**Comparative and superlative forms of adjectives and adverbs**)

98. lighter (**Comparative and superlative forms of adjectives and adverbs**)

99. least experienced (**Comparative and superlative forms of adjectives and adverbs**)

100. fastest (**Comparative and superlative forms of adjectives and adverbs**)

101. older (**Comparative and superlative forms of adjectives and adverbs**)

102. better (**Comparative and superlative forms of adjectives and adverbs**)

103. better (**Comparative and superlative forms of adjectives and adverbs**)

104. faster (**Comparative and superlative forms of adjectives and adverbs**)

105. most carefully (**Comparative and superlative forms of adjectives and adverbs**)

106. Later (**Choosing the correct conjunctive adverb**)

107. subsequently (**Choosing the correct conjunctive adverb**)

108. Besides (**Choosing the correct conjunctive adverb**)

109. Conversely (**Choosing the correct conjunctive adverb**)

110. Consequently (**Choosing the correct conjunctive adverb**)

111. however (**Choosing the correct conjunctive adverb**)

112. Therefore **(Choosing the correct conjunctive adverb)**

113. first **(Choosing the correct conjunctive adverb)**

114. Similarly **(Choosing the correct conjunctive adverb)**

115. also **(Choosing the correct conjunctive adverb)**

116. certainly **(Choosing the correct conjunctive adverb)**

Grade Yourself

Circle the numbers of the questions you missed, then fill in the total incorrect for each topic. If you answered more than three questions incorrectly, you need to focus on that topic. (If a topic has less than three questions and you had at least one wrong, we suggest you study that topic also. Read your textbook, a review book, or ask your teacher for help.)

Subject: Adjectives and Adverbs

Topic	Question Numbers	Number Incorrect
Types of adjectives	1, 2, 3, 4, 5, 6, 7, 8, 9, 10	
Use of adjectives in sentences	11, 12, 13, 14, 15, 16, 17, 18, 19, 20	
Adverbs	21, 22, 23, 24, 25, 26, 27, 28, 29, 30, 31, 32, 33, 34, 35, 36, 37, 38, 39, 40	
Negatives	41, 42, 43, 44, 45, 46, 47, 48, 49, 50	
Choosing adjectives or adverbs	51, 52, 53, 54, 55, 56, 57, 58, 59, 60, 61, 62, 63, 64, 65, 66, 67, 68, 69, 70, 71, 72, 73, 74, 75, 76, 77, 78, 79, 80	
Comparative and superlative forms of adjectives and adverbs	81, 82, 83, 84, 85, 86, 87, 88, 89, 90, 91, 92, 93, 94, 95, 96, 97, 98, 99 100, 101, 102, 103, 104, 105	
Choosing the correct conjunctive adverb	106, 107, 108, 109, 110, 111, 112, 113, 114, 115, 116	

Conjunctions

  Test Yourself

7.1 Coordinating Conjunctions

Coordinating conjunctions indicate relationships between words and phrases and between sentences. *And* indicates addition. *Or* indicates alternative. *But* indicates a contrast or *to the contrary*. *Yet* means *although* or *nevertheless*. *For* indicates *because*; it is used to join two sentences where the effect comes before the cause. *So* means *therefore*; it is used to join two sentences where the cause comes before the effect.

Elements joined by coordinating conjunctions must be parallel grammatically.

In the following sentences, choose the coordinating conjunction in parentheses that logically joins the two sentences.

1. In his essay "Shame," Dick Gregory narrates a childhood incident (and/or) describes its effect on him.

2. Gregory's teacher knew he was poor, (and/but) she thought he was stupid.

3. He could not think clearly in class, (for/so) he had not eaten breakfast.

4. He was so hungry he would sometimes eat paste, (but/or) he would steal a bite of another kid's lunch.

5. He was in love with Helene Tucker, (and/for) she was pretty, clean and smart.

6. Helene's father was a paperhanger, (so/yet) her family was provided for.

7. Gregory's family had no money to spare, (so/yet) he had three dollars he earned shining shoes.

8. The teacher asked the class how much each person's father would contribute to the Community Chest, (but/for) she did not call on Dick.

9. She said Dick's family was on welfare (and/so) he would not have money to contribute.

10. The money was being collected for families like his, (and/but), she added, he did not have a father.

Rewrite the following sentences to correct any errors in parallelism in elements joined by coordinating conjunctions. Some of the sentences are correct as *written*.

11. To order the amazing Vego-Wiz-O, use a credit card or send a check.

12. Call immediately to receive a gift worth at least $1.29 and start enjoying your Wiz-O at once.

13. The Wiz-O is great for chopping onions and to slice potatoes.

14. Stainless-steel knives can be cleaned easily, but they are difficult to sharpen.

15. Low-carbon-steel knives attract stains, but they can be sharpened easily and cheap.

16. Lee enjoys cooking but not to wash dishes.

17. Rhoda dislikes housework, yet she enjoys having a clean house.

18. The Suckup Vacuum will clean your rug, dust your walls, or used for freshening your draperies.

19. Use the hottest setting on the clothes dryer for towels and if the clothes are cotton.

20. A joke says a clean desk is the sign of not enough work to do or having a sick mind.

7.2 Correlative Conjunctions

Correlative conjunctions use a pair of words to indicate relationships between words, phrases, and sentences. Correlative conjunctions can be used to join independent clauses to form a single sentence. The placement of correlative conjunctions is determined by the meaning of the sentence.

Elements joined by correlative conjunctions must be parallel grammatically.

The correlative conjunctions are: *both/and, either/or, neither/nor*; *whether/or*, and *not only/but also*.

Choose the correlative conjunctions that logically complete the meaning of the sentence to fill in the blanks.

21. There are two tests for the truth of a categorical syllogism :_____ the major premise _____ the minor premise must be true.

22. For a syllogism to be sound, _____ must the premises be true _____ the syllogism must be valid.

23. Validity is tested by seeing _____ the syllogism follows the correct form _____ how the terms are arranged.

24. The major premise of a disjunctive syllogism presents alternatives: _____ A exists, _____ B exists.

25. The data for inductive reasoning are derived _____ from experience _____ observation.

26. The generalizations derived from inductive reasoning cannot be proved true; they can provide _____ certainty _____ inevitability.

27. _____ the data may not provide sufficient examples, _____ it may be impossible to examine all instances.

28. _____ is the study of logic interesting ____ it _____ helps one detect false claims in advertising.

29. An ad for mouthwash, for example, may imply _____ you buy our product _____ no one will want to kiss you.

30. _____ you are kissed _____ you are not kissed does not depend on the brand of mouthwash you use.

7.3 Subordinating Conjunctions

Subordinating conjunctions are used to join dependent clauses to other clauses in a sentence. They indicate relationships such as cause and effect, comparison and contrast, time, possibility, and location. A subordinate clause begins with a subordinating conjunction. Clauses that begin with subordinating conjunctions can function as adverbs or nouns.

Examples:

Immigrants become more confident when they learn to speak English well.

When they learn to speak English well is a subordinate clause functioning as an adverb because it modifies the verb "learn."

> Hassan knows where he can register for an English class.
>
> *Where he can register for an English class* is a subordinate clause functioning as a noun because it is the object of the verb *knows*.

Underline the subordinate clause in each of the following sentences.

31. Before Assam learned to speak English, he felt lost in the United States.

32. He had come to this country when he was sixteen years old.

33. SuLai had learned English because it was a required subject in her native country.

34. Although English seems easy to native speakers, its idioms can be confusing.

35. Choosing the correct definite or indefinite article may be difficult if English is not your native language.

36. Where adverbs are placed in sentences can also cause problems.

37. Native English speakers may have similar difficulties if they try to learn another language.

38. Whenever Bob read German, he waited for the verb that appears at the end of the sentence.

39. Some languages use a prepositional phrase for possessives, while in English possession can be indicated by the use of an apostrophe.

40. For English speakers, learning languages that do not use the Roman alphabet is more difficult than learning the Romance languages.

Identify the subordinate clause in each sentence as a noun clause or an adverb clause.

41. Tom the Piper's son ran away after he stole a pig.

42. Wherever little Mary went, her lamb was sure to go.

43. Mary was annoyed since the lamb became a pest.

44. Although Jack Sprat ate no fat, he was overweight.

45. Because he indulged in sugary candy, he gained pounds.

46. While Mrs. Sprat ate no lean, she exercised often and remained thin.

47. Little Miss Muffett didn't know how the spider found her.

48. Why Mary Contrary's garden contained silver bells and cockle shells, no one knew.

49. If those grew in your garden, you would be amazed.

50. When Peter Peter Pumpkin Eater put his wife in a pumpkin shell, he was acting like a male chauvinist.

7.4 Relative Clauses

Relative pronouns that introduce subordinate clauses act as subordinating conjunctions.

Relative clauses can function as nouns or adjectives.

Examples:

> Whichever store has the lowest prices will attract the most customers.

Whichever store has the lowest prices is a subordinate clause beginning with a relative pronoun. It functions as a noun because it is the subject of the verb *will attract*.

A Polaroid camera, which provides immediate prints, makes it possible to enjoy the scene and the picture of it at the same time.

Which provides immediate prints is a subordinate clause beginning with a relative pronoun. It functions as an adjective because it modifies *camera*.

A restrictive clause provides information that is required to identify or define the word or words it modifies. It is not set off by commas.

Example:

Photographers who forget to advance the film in the camera take double exposures.

A nonrestrictive clause is not needed to identify the word or words it modifies; the sentence would make sense if the clause was omitted. It is set off by commas.

Example:

Harry, who is a photographer, needed some film and flashbulbs for his camera.

Indicate whether the relative clause in the following sentences functions as a noun or an adjective.

51. What Harry found in the box containing his Christmas present surprised him.

52. He did not know that his friend Myrna was aware of his interest in photography.

53. She had bought him a light meter that was better than the one he owned.

54. Myrna, who was very thoughtful, had learned of Harry's hobby by asking his brother about it.

55. Alfred Eisenstaedt took a famous photograph that showed a sailor kissing a nurse to celebrate the end of World War II.

56. Whoever sees that picture feels the joy of that moment.

57. Margaret Bourke-White was a journalist and photographer who covered the Second World War.

58. Walker Evans took the photographs that appeared in James Agee's book *Let Us Now Praise Famous Men*.

59. Humphrey Bogart won a Best Actor Oscar for his role in *The African Queen*, a film Agee wrote the screenplay for.

60. Edward Steichen was a photographer who had studied painting.

If the relative clause in the following sentences is non-restrictive, add the necessary commas. If the relative clause is restrictive, do not change the sentence.

61. Ann's husband who is a teacher arrives home at 4:00 P.M. on weekdays.

62. People who died before 1930 never heard of pantyhose, VCRs, or penicillin.

63. Tanya's house which is on a busy street is always noisy.

64. Roberto's dream house which he doesn't think he'll ever be able to afford, overlooks the ocean and has a fireplace in the bedroom.

65. The hurricane that struck Bermuda caused much damage.

66. Houses that are not shaded by trees can be expensive to cool.

67. Houses near the beach which are often expensive are cooled by sea breezes.

68. Symptoms like fever and body aches which occur with the flu cause discomfort.

69. Symptoms that occur with the flu include fever and body aches.

70. Automobiles that have four-wheel drive can go over rough terrain.

71. Pip's unknown benefactor whoever he or she was paid for his education.

72. Dickens whose childhood was harsh wrote about children in difficult circumstances.

73. Tiny Tim who was loved by his family was crippled.

74. The ghosts that haunt Ebenezer Scrooge cause a change in his character.

75. The children who attend Mr. Gradgrind's school in *Hard Times* are taught only facts.

76. Andrea whose brother had gone to summer camp was lonely.

77. A trifle whatever it may be seems like an odd name for a food.

78. A trifle is a dessert that is popular in Great Britain.

79. A trifle whatever else it may contain always includes custard.

80. Lassie who has a feminine name was played by a male dog in the film *Lassie Come Home*.

 # Check Yourself

1. and (**Coordinating conjunctions**)

2. and (**Coordinating conjunctions**)

3. for (**Coordinating conjunctions**)

4. or (**Coordinating conjunctions**)

5. for (**Coordinating conjunctions**)

6. so (**Coordinating conjunctions**)

7. yet (**Coordinating conjunctions**)

8. but (**Coordinating conjunctions**)

9. so (**Coordinating conjunctions**)

10. and (**Coordinating conjunctions**)

11. correct (**Parallel elements with coordinating conjunctions**)

12. correct (**Parallel elements with coordinating conjunctions**)

13. The Wiz-O is great for chopping onions and for slicing potatoes. (**Parallel elements with coordinating conjunctions**)

14. correct (**Parallel elements with coordinating conjunctions**)

15. Low-carbon-steel knives attract stains, but they can be sharpened easily and cheaply. (**Parallel elements with coordinating conjunctions**)

16. Lee enjoys cooking but not washing dishes. (**Parallel elements with coordinating conjunctions**)

17. correct (**Parallel elements with coordinating conjunctions**)

18. The Suckup Vacuum will clean your rug, dust your walls, or freshen your draperies. (**Parallel elements with coordinating conjunctions**)

19. Use the hottest setting on the clothes dryer for towels and for cotton clothes. (**Parallel elements with coordinating conjunctions**)

20. A joke says a clean desk is a sign of not having enough to do or of having a sick mind. (**Parallel elements with coordinating conjunctions**)

21. both/and (**Correlative conjunctions**)

22. not only/but also (**Correlative conjunctions**)

23. whether/or (**Correlative conjunctions**)

24. either/or (**Correlative conjunctions**)

25. both/and—either/or would also be correct (**Correlative conjunctions**)

26. neither/nor (**Correlative conjunctions**)

27. either/or (**Correlative conjunctions**)

28. not only/but also (**Correlative conjunctions**)

29. either/or (**Correlative conjunctions**)

30. whether/or (**Correlative conjunctions**)

31. Before Assam learned to speak English (**Identifying subordinate clauses**)

32. when he was sixteen years old (**Identifying subordinate clauses**)

33. because it was a required subject in her native country (**Identifying subordinate clauses**)

34. Although English seems easy to native speakers (**Identifying subordinate clauses**)

35. if English is not your native language (**Identifying subordinate clauses**)

36. Where adverbs are placed in sentences (**Identifying subordinate clauses**)

37. if they try to learn another language (**Identifying subordinate clauses**)

38. Whenever Bob reads German (**Identifying subordinate clauses**)

39. while in English possession can be indicated by an apostrophe (**Identifying subordinate clauses**)

40. that do not use the Roman alphabet (**Identifying subordinate clauses**)

41. after he stole a pig: adverb—modifies *ran* (**Functions of subordinate clauses**)

42. Wherever little Mary went: noun—subject of sentence (**Functions of subordinate clauses**)

43. since the lamb became a pest: adverb—modifies *was annoyed* (**Functions of subordinate clauses**)

44. Although Jack Sprat ate no fat: adverb—modifies *was overweight* (**Functions of subordinate clauses**)

45. Because he indulged in sugary candies: adverb—modifies *gained* (**Functions of subordinate clauses**)

46. While Mrs. Sprat ate no lean: adverb—modifies *exercised* (**Functions of subordinate clauses**)

47. how the spider found her: noun—object of verb *know* (**Functions of subordinate clauses**)

48. Why Mary Contrary's garden contained silver bells and cockle shells: noun—object of verb *knew* (**Functions of subordinate clauses**)

49. If they grew in your garden: adverb—modifies *would be amazed* (**Functions of subordinate clauses**)

50. When Peter Peter Pumpkin Eater put his wife in a pumpkin shell: adverb—modifies *was acting* (**Functions of subordinate clauses**)

51. What Harry found in the box containing his Christmas present: noun—subject of verb *surprised* (**Functions of relative clauses**)

52. that his friend Myrna was aware of his interest in photography: noun—object of verb *know* (**Functions of relative clauses**)

53. that was better than the one he owned: adjective—modifies *meter* (**Functions of relative clauses**)

54. who was very thoughtful: adjective—modifies *Myrna* (**Functions of relative clauses**)

55. that showed a sailor kissing a nurse to celebrate the end of World War II: adjective—modifies *picture* (**Functions of relative clauses**)

56. Whoever sees that picture: noun—subject of verb *feels* (**Functions of relative clauses**)

57. who covered the Second World War: adjective—modifies subject *Margaret Bourke-White* (**Functions of relative clauses**)

58. that appeared in James Agee's book *Let Us Now Praise Famous Men*: adjective—modifies *photographs* (**Functions of relative clauses**)

59. that Agee wrote the screenplay for: adjective—modifies *film* (**Functions of relative clauses**)

60. who had studied painting: adjective—modifies *photographer* (**Functions of relative clauses**)

61. Ann's husband, who is a teacher, arrives home at 4:00 P.M. on weekdays. (**Restrictive and nonrestrictive clauses**)

62. correct (**Restrictive and nonrestrictive clauses**)

63. Tanya's home, which is on a busy street, is noisy. (**Restrictive and nonrestrictive clauses**)

64. Roberto's dream house, which he doesn't think he'll ever be able to afford, overlooks the ocean and has a fireplace in the bedroom. (**Restrictive and nonrestrictive clauses**)

65. correct (**Restrictive and nonrestrictive clauses**)

66. correct (**Restrictive and nonrestrictive clauses**)

67. Houses near the beach, which are often expensive, are cooled by sea breezes. (**Restrictive and nonrestrictive clauses**)

68. Symptoms like fever and body aches, which occur with the flu, cause discomfort. (**Restrictive and nonrestrictive clauses**)

69. correct (**Restrictive and nonrestrictive clauses**)

70. correct (**Restrictive and nonrestrictive clauses**)

71. Pip's unknown benefactor, whoever he or she was, paid for his education. (**Restrictive and nonrestrictive clauses**)

72. Dickens, whose childhood was hard, wrote about children in difficult circumstances. (**Restrictive and nonrestrictive clauses**)

73. Tiny Tim, who was loved by his family, was crippled. (**Restrictive and nonrestrictive clauses**)

74. correct (**Restrictive and nonrestrictive clauses**)

75. correct (**Restrictive and nonrestrictive clauses**)

76. Andrea, whose brother had gone to summer camp, was lonely. (**Restrictive and nonrestrictive clauses**)

77. A trifle, whatever it may be, seems like an odd name for a food. (**Restrictive and nonrestrictive clauses**)

78. correct (**Restrictive and nonrestrictive clauses**)

79. A trifle, whatever else it may contain, always includes custard. (**Restrictive and nonrestrictive clauses**)

80. Lassie, who has a feminine name, was played by a male dog in the film *Lassie Come Home*. (**Restrictive and nonrestrictive clauses**)

Grade Yourself

Circle the numbers of the questions you missed, then fill in the total incorrect for each topic. If you answered more than three questions incorrectly, you need to focus on that topic. (If a topic has less than three questions and you had at least one wrong, we suggest you study that topic also. Read your textbook, a review book, or ask your teacher for help.)

Subject: Conjunctions

Topic	Question Numbers	Number Incorrect
Coordinating conjunctions	1, 2, 3, 4, 5, 6, 7, 8, 9, 10	
Parallel elements with coordinating conjunctions	11, 12, 13, 14, 15, 16, 17, 18, 19, 20,	
Correlative conjunctions	21, 22, 23, 24, 25, 26, 27, 28, 29, 30	
Identifying subordinate clauses	31, 32, 33, 34, 35, 36, 37, 38, 39, 40	
Functions of subordinate clauses	41, 42, 43, 44, 45, 46, 47, 48, 49, 50	
Functions of relative clauses	51, 52, 53, 54, 55, 56, 57, 58, 59, 60	
Restrictive and nonrestrictive clauses	61, 62, 63, 64, 65, 66, 67, 68, 69, 70, 71, 72, 73, 74, 75, 76, 77, 78, 79, 80	

Prepositions

8

8.1 Identifying Simple and Compound Prepositions

Simple and compound prepositions indicate relationships between nouns, pronouns, and other words in sentences. Most simple prepositions are short words such as *from*, *to*, *under*, and *with*. Compound prepositions are phrases made up of prepositions and other words.

Examples:

apart from, in spite of, next to

Underline the simple or compound prepositions in the paragraph below. There are ten prepositions.

1-10. The partial handwritten manuscript of *Huckleberry Finn* was lost for many years. According to scholars, there were differences between the manuscript and the published version. In one episode Twain omitted from the novel, Jim tells Huck about a time when he saw a ghost. Jim explains his master was a medical student who asked him to move a corpse onto a dissecting table. Jim placed the corpse on the table. When it rolled off the table, Jim thought it was a ghost.

8.2 Prepositional Phrases in Sentences

Prepositional phrases can function as adjectives or adverbs.

Prepositional phrases should usually be placed close to the words they modify.

Identify the prepositional phrase in the sentence. If it functions as an adjective, write AJ. If it functions as and adverb, write AV.

11. *Jurassic Park*'s scenes of a violent nature may frighten young children.

12. Until recently, dinosaurs were thought to be clumsy.

13. Scientists have changed their views about the dinosaurs' agility.

14. In spite of their wings, the pterosaursus species are classified as reptiles.

15. Eohippus, unlike the modern horse, was quite small.

16. Ferns were some of the earliest plant species.

17. Under pressure and heat, decayed vegetation may form coal.

A prepositional phrase in each sentence is misplaced. Rewrite the sentence so that it is not confusing or unintentionally funny.

18. The suspect was described as a six-foot-tall man with a heavy beard weighing 180 pounds.

19. The realtor sold the house to the Smith family that had leaky plumbing.

72

20. Robert cooked steaks for the children with barbeque sauce on them,

21. Laura borrowed a bicycle from a friend with a basket.

22. Professor Delgado made it clear why plagiarism is wrong on Monday.

23. News headline: "Two Men Found Slain by Six-Year-Old Are Identified."

24. A property owner has filed a request to fill in a wetland with the Corps of Engineers.

25. Ilsa was engaged to a man with a Porsche named Hans.

26. The game warden noticed a mountain lion in his truck while driving through the San Gabriel Mountains.

27. Shirley Jackson wrote a controversial short story about a ritual in a village called "The Lottery."

8.3 Restrictive and Nonrestrictive Prepositional Phrases

Set off nonrestrictive prepositional phrases with commas. Do not use commas around restrictive prepositional phrases.

In the following sentences, add commas where necessary to set off nonrestrictive prepositional phrases.

28. New medical technologies with their high level of sophistication help save lives.

29. Genetic engineering according to many physicians is still controversial.

30. Doctors with doubts about its safety may use more conservative treatments.

31. The syringes inside the autoclave are heated to kill microbes and bacteria.

32. Aspirin in use for a long time has effects that are well documented.

33. Band-Aids like aspirin are found in most home medicine cabinets.

34. Band-Aids out of their original wrappings can not be guaranteed to be sterile.

35. The shelves of the medicine cabinet are made of glass.

36. The many cold remedies at the pharmacy all have similar ingredients.

37. Each manufacturer through advertising tries to convince consumers to buy its brand.

8.4 Correct Usage of Prepositional Phrases

Prepositions are idiomatic. Consult a usage handbook or dictionary to ensure you use the correct preposition; do not omit necessary prepositions, and do not include unnecessary prepositions.

In the following sentences, write the correct choice of the two prepositions in parentheses.

38. Many Americans have feelings of great pride (for/in) the American flag.

39. A proposed constitutional amendment will prohibit disrespect (for/of) the flag.

40. Senator Verna voted in opposition (of/to) the finance bill.

41. She was not in agreement (to/with) her party's leadership.

42. (On/to) the contrary, Senator Okada voted for it.

43. He relied (in/on) the leadership's good judgment.

44. Ken was a participant (in/of) the voter registration program.

45. The program stressed the importance (in/of) voting in all elections.

46. The Republican Party's platform is different (from/than) the Democratic Party's platform.

47. Susan was disrespectful (of/to) her sister.

48. Anna was not angry (at/on) her.

49. There's no need (for/to) lose you temper.

50. Sara and Janet agreed to divide the tasks (among/between) the two of them.

51. (At/on) Saturday, the house will be cleaned.

52. The concert will begin (at/on) 7:30 P.M.

53. The Boston Pops Orchestra will play (at/in) Central Park.

54. Bring lawn chairs, unless you want to sit(in/on) the grass.

55. A trifle is a dessert that consists (in/of) cake, custard, fruit, and whipped cream.

56. Franklin could not choose (among/between) the many delicious-looking pastries on the dessert cart.

57. The waiter took the dishes(off/off of) the counter and placed them on the tray.

58. Jan walked over (at/to) the buffet.

59. Artificial sweeteners are substitutes (for/to)sugar.

60. Simon's Lemonade is free (for/of) artificial flavorings.

61. Professor Leroux's interest centered (around/on) women's role in American history.

62. I couldn't remember (where/where at) Red's Toy Shop was.

63. Stan told me it was (at/in) Church Street and Second Avenue.

64. It's closer (at/to)my house than I thought it was.

65. Red's doesn't open (at/until) noon.

66. The owner moved the display (out/out of) the window.

67. Don't throw trash (out/out of) the car window.

68. Wait (on/until) getting to a trash can before tossing out the hamburger wrapper.

69. The defense attorney objected (at/to) the prosecutor's question.

70. In 1558, Elizabeth I was crowned queen (in/of) England.

71. Ruth Bader Ginsburg was appointed Justice (in/of) the United States Supreme Court in 1994.

72. Two sides of a regular pentagon are parallel (to/with) one other.

73. The base angles of an isosceles triangle are equal (to/through) each other.

74. All the angles of an equilateral triangle are identical (to/with) one another.

75. When a picture is drawn in perspective, an object's size is proportional (from/to) its distance from an observer.

76. Can I rely (in/on) your ability to keep a secret?

77. Jose waited (for/on) an opportunity to explain his views.

Check Yourself

1. of (**Identifying prepositions**)

2. for (**Identifying prepositions**)

3. According to (**Identifying prepositions**)

4. between (**Identifying prepositions**)

5. In (**Identifying prepositions**)

6. from (**Identifying prepositions**)

7. about (**Identifying prepositions**)

8. onto (**Identifying prepositions**)

9. on (**Identifying prepositions**)

10. off (**Identifying prepositions**)

11. AJ: *of a violent nature* modifies *scenes.* (**Functions of prepositional phrases**)

12. AV: *Until recently* modifies *were thought.* (**Functions of prepositional phrases**)

13. AJ: *about dinosaurs' agility* modifies *views.* (**Functions of prepositional phrases**)

14. AJ: *In spite of their wings* modifies *pterosaurus.* (**Functions of prepositional phrases**)

15. AJ: *unlike the modern horse* modifies *Eohippus.* (**Functions of prepositional phrases**)

16. AJ: *of the earliest* modifies *species.* (**Functions of prepositional phrases**)

17. AJ: *Under pressure and heat* modifies *vegetation.* (**Functions of prepositional phrases**)

18. The suspect was described as a six-foot-tall man, weighing 180 pounds, with a beard. (**Misplaced prepositional phrases**)

19. The realtor sold the house that had leaky plumbing to the Smith family. (**Misplaced prepositional phrases**)

20. Robert cooked steaks with barbecue sauce on them for the children. (**Misplaced prepositional phrases**)

21. Laura borrowed a bicycle with a basket from a friend. (**Misplaced prepositional phrases**)

22. Professor Delgado made it clear on Monday why plagiarism is wrong. (**Misplaced prepositional phrases**)

23. News headline: "Two Men Found Slain Are Identified by Six-Year-Old." (**Misplaced prepositional phrases**)

24. A property owner has filed a request with the Corps of Engineers to fill in a wetland. (**Misplaced prepositional phrases**)

25. Ilsa was engaged to Hans, a man with a Porsche. (**Misplaced prepositional phrases**)

26. The game warden, while driving in his truck through the San Gabriel Mountains, noticed a mountain lion. (**Misplaced prepositional phrases**)

27. Shirley Jackson wrote a controversial short story called "The Lottery" about a ritual in a village. (**Restrictive and nonrestrictive prepositional phrases**)

28. New medical technologies, with their high level of sophistication, help save lives. (**Restrictive and nonrestrictive prepositional phrases**)

29. Genetic engineering, according to many physicians, is still controversial. (**Restrictive and nonrestrictive prepositional phrases**)

30. no commas needed (**Restrictive and nonrestrictive prepositional phrases**)

31. no commas needed (**Restrictive and nonrestrictive prepositional phrases**)

32. Aspirin, in use for a long time, has effects that are well documented. (**Restrictive and nonrestrictive prepositional phrases**)

33. Band-Aids, like aspirin, are found in most home medicine chests. (**Restrictive and nonrestrictive prepositional phrases**)

34. no commas needed (**Restrictive and nonrestrictive prepositional phrases**)

35. no commas needed (**Restrictive and nonrestrictive prepositional phrases**)

36. no commas needed (**Restrictive and nonrestrictive prepositional phrases**)

37. Each cold remedy manufacturer, through advertising, tries to convince consumers to buy its product. (**Restrictive and nonrestrictive prepositional phrases**)

38. in (**Correct usage of prepositional phrases**)

39. for (**Correct usage of prepositional phrases**)

40. to (**Correct usage of prepositional phrases**)

41. with (**Correct usage of prepositional phrases**)

42. On the contrary (**Correct usage of prepositional phrases**)

43. on (**Correct usage of prepositional phrases**)

44. in (**Correct usage of prepositional phrases**)

45. of (**Correct usage of prepositional phrases**)

46. from (**Correct usage of prepositional phrases**)

47. of (**Correct usage of prepositional phrases**)

48. at (**Correct usage of prepositional phrases**)

49. to (**Correct usage of prepositional phrases**)

50. between **(Correct usage of prepositional phrases)**

51. On **(Correct usage of prepositional phrases)**

52. at **(Correct usage of prepositional phrases)**

53. in **(Correct usage of prepositional phrases)**

54. on **(Correct usage of prepositional phrases)**

55. of **(Correct usage of prepositional phrases)**

56. among **(Correct usage of prepositional phrases)**

57. off **(Correct usage of prepositional phrases)**

58. to **(Correct usage of prepositional phrases)**

59. for **(Correct usage of prepositional phrases)**

60. of **(Correct usage of prepositional phrases)**

61. on **(Correct usage of prepositional phrases)**

62. where **(Correct usage of prepositional phrases)**

63. at **(Correct usage of prepositional phrases)**

64. to **(Correct usage of prepositional phrases)**

65. until **(Correct usage of prepositional phrases)**

66. out of **(Correct usage of prepositional phrases)**

67. out **(Correct usage of prepositional phrases)**

68. until **(Correct usage of prepositional phrases)**

69. to **(Correct usage of prepositional phrases)**

70. of **(Correct usage of prepositional phrases)**

71. of **(Correct usage of prepositional phrases)**

72. to **(Correct usage of prepositional phrases)**

73. to **(Correct usage of prepositional phrases)**

74. with **(Correct usage of prepositional phrases)**

75. to **(Correct usage of prepositional phrases)**

76. on **(Correct usage of prepositional phrases)**

77. for **(Correct usage of prepositional phrases)**

Grade Yourself

Circle the numbers of the questions you missed, then fill in the total incorrect for each topic. If you answered more than three questions incorrectly, you need to focus on that topic. (If a topic has less than three questions and you had at least one wrong, we suggest you study that topic also. Read your textbook, a review book, or ask your teacher for help.)

Subject: Prepositions

Topic	Question Numbers	Number Incorrect
Identifying prepositions	1, 2, 3, 4, 5, 6, 7, 8, 9, 10	
Functions of prepositional phrases	11, 12, 13, 14, 15, 16, 17	
Misplaced prepositional phrases	18, 19, 20, 21, 22, 23, 24, 25, 26	
Restrictive and nonrestrictive prepositional phrases	27, 28, 29, 30, 31, 32, 33, 34, 35, 36, 37	
Correct usage of prepositional phrases	38, 39, 40, 41, 42, 43, 44, 45, 46, 47, 48, 49, 50, 51, 52, 53, 54, 55, 56, 57, 58, 59, 60, 61, 62, 63, 64, 65, 66, 67, 68, 69, 70, 71, 72, 73, 74, 75, 76, 77	

Final Examination

9

Brief Yourself

To the students: No final examination will cover all the subtopics in this book. Consult your instructor about what material your examination will include. This final examination includes the subtopics in grammar that most frequently cause problems in students' writing.

Test Yourself

Section 1:   Uses of the Comma

Rewrite any sentences in which commas need to be added or in which commas are used improperly. Some of the sentences are correct.

1. Jeff who is eighteen is now driving the family car.

2. The artist who gave me that painting has moved to Wyoming.

3. John usually arrives to class on time, he plans for possible delays.

4. Dinah is always late for the meeting, so let's begin without her.

5. The car, an old clunker, has rust spots and dents.

6. Tamiko is driving it, and she looks upset.

7. Scientists with an interest in studying insects are called entomologists.

8. Rap music with its insistent beat can become monotonous.

9. Jean Paul Sartre the existentialist philosopher was also a playwright.

10. *Sophie's World*, by Jostein Gaarder, is a novel but it is also a history of Western philosophy.

11. Many of the conversations between Sophie and her tutor that occur in the novel sound like Socratic dialogues.

12. The pre-Socratic Greek philosophers among whom are Thales and Heraclitus begin Sophie's lessons.

13. *Siddhartha* was written by a Westerner yet its philosophy is Eastern.

14. An unabridged dictionary which is usually expensive can be a good investment.

15. But the *Oxford English Dictionary* a multivolume classic is impractical for home use.

16. However, scholars who need to know the history of a word's use consult it frequently.

17. Encyclopedias, that once took up much shelf space, now appear on a single CD-ROM disk.

18. A thesaurus, in spite of its usefulness can create problems.

19. Users may choose a word with incorrect connotations or they may select words that do not fit the context.

20. Beware of the thesaurus, it can be a dangerous beast.

Section 2: Correcting Sentence Fragments

Rewrite the following paragraph to correct any sentence fragments. Some of the sentences are correct.

21-30.

"The Lottery," by Shirley Jackson, is a horror story. That begins in sunshine and ends in violence. And it is more. The people of the town maintain an old tradition. Clinging to a ritual whose meaning and purpose are not understood. Which makes the lottery senseless. Cruel and barbaric. Because the little boy participates in stoning his mother to death. Readers are appalled. Yet having different interpretations of the story's meaning.

Section 3: Agreement

Correct any errors in agreement in the following sentences. Some of the sentences are correct.

31. Anti-discrimination laws has given equal opportunity to job seekers.

32. Each of the new nations will have their own constitution.

33. Those suggestions sounds like nonsense to me.

34. Everyone has her or his favorite kind of music.

35. The road to success and victory was plagued by many problems.

36. Although wool carpeting is expensive, they wear well.

37. It is difficult to follow instructions when it isn't written clearly.

38. Everyone has their own opinion about how to solve the problem.

39. There is the keys that Kent misplaced.

40. Because of budget cuts, either the recreation program or the library suffers.

41. Some tortoises are long-lived; it may live for one hundred years.

42. When someone suddenly hears a loud noise, they may jump.

43. The O'Haras and the Parks shares a cabin every summer.

44. To prevent injury, the protection football players use include shoulder pads, knee pads, mouthpieces, and helmets.

45. On a road trip, the team wears gray uniforms.

46. At home games, the players wear white uniforms.

47. Neither Min's cat nor his dog sleep outdoors.

48. In a stunning upset, the number-one team got their tail kicked.

49. Both Emily and Valerie enjoy Bizet's opera *Carmen*.

50. The motive for Jim's actions surprise Trish.

Section 4: Misplaced and Dangling Elements

Rewrite the following sentences to correct any errors caused by misplaced or dangling elements. Some of the sentences are correct.

51. When heated, Rayna begins curling my hair.

52. The waffle iron being heated enough, Mike pours the batter on it.

53. A huge boulder fell as we rounded the corner with a crash.

54. Salted or plain, Hank find peanuts delicious.

55. Watching T.V. all evening, the dirty dishes were still on the table.

56. The text that Joseph carefully studied explained the answer.

57. I read that the murderer had been caught in the newspaper.

58. Hopping from branch to branch in the trees, Valerie saw the squirrels in the park.

59. Uninterested in boys, Carol's adolescence was tranquil.

60. While waiting in line to pay, the checker bagged my groceries.

61. Worried by financial problems, a better job was what Anne needed.

62. Stop at a red traffic signal when it is flashing.

63. Carrying a heavy suitcase, the walk from the ticket counter to the gate seemed very long.

64. The problem that Karen examined thoroughly confused her.

65. Sean read in *Time* magazine that a gene helping to cause Alzheimer's disease has been discovered.

66. Excited about the championship, a celebration was held in the locker room.

67. When flashing, do not pass a yellow traffic signal.

68. Shortly after being seated, the waiter approached our table.

69. While waiting to buy tickets, Ned wondered if any good seats were left.

70. The news article that Myra glanced at quickly explained the complicated situations.

Section 5: Parallel Elements

Correct any errors in parallelism in the following sentences. Some of the sentences are correct.

71. In *The Grapes of Wrath*, the Joads are forced to leave their home when the crops fail and the bank's bulldozer tractors over their house.

72. To hope for a better life and anticipating California will be paradise, they set out on their journey.

73. The dealers selling used cars that the migrants need for their journey pretend to help them but sucker them into buying junk.

74. Underpowered, overloaded, and with a leak, the engines break down.

75. Their temporary settlements, where the migrants lived in tents or cardboard shacks, sleeping on the ground, and cooked over open fires, were called Hoovervilles.

76. Ruthie and Winfield, the two youngest Joad children, had never seen a flush toilet or a shower until they arrived at Weedpatch Camp.

77. After he accidentally kills a man, Tom Joad can run from the law or hiding with his family.

78. The migrants find pleasure and amusement in telling stories and jokes, playing the harmonica, guitar, or fiddle, and to dance.

79. When the migrants arrive in California, they are cheated, despised, and people harass them.

80. Yet because of their spiritual strength, strong family ties, and refusal to admit defeat, they endure.

81. In a song popular during World War II, Americans sang about praising the Lord and pass the ammunition.

82. The worker in "Old Man River" is tired of living and scared to die.

83. Slaves while working sang to lighten the burden of labor and to express feelings they hid from their masters.

84. Rap music uses strong rhythm, chants, and rhymes.

85. The strings of a violin can be bowed, plucked, or strum them.

86. Hot, cool and the blues: the moods of jazz vary.

87. Background music in films is used to create suspense, set a mood, and to illuminate characters.

88. "Moshing" involves physical crowding, hand slapping, and body bumping.

89. Michael Jackson's "moonwalk" displays gliding, stooping, and to reverse direction.

90. Emily, when exercising, enjoys calisthenics but not to jog.

Section 6:   Shifts

Correct any shifts in pronouns or verb tense in the following sentences. Some of the sentences are correct.

91-100.

Some students do not realize how much time it takes to write a research paper. They require several preliminary steps. They choose a subject and restricted its focus. Then you need to find relevant materials in the library. Both books and periodicals were used in many research papers. Next they take notes. Then you must organize the notes. At this point, an outline of the paper is helpful. At last it was time to draft the paper, but you must also leave enough time to revise and edit it. Finally, one must compile a list of works cited. Then they typed it before the due date.

Check Yourself

1. Jeff, who is eighteen, is now driving the family car. (restrictive and nonrestrictive clauses

2. correct (**Restrictive and nonrestrictive clauses**)

3. John usually arrives to class on time; he plans for possible delays. (**Fused sentences**)

4. correct (**Compound sentences**)

5. correct (**Appositives**)

6. correct (**Compound sentences**)

7. correct (**Restrictive and nonrestrictive prepositional phrases**)

8. Rap music, with its insistent beat, can be monotonous. (**Restrictive and nonrestrictive prepositional phrases**)

9. Jean Paul Sartre, the existentialist philosopher, was also a playwright. (**Appositives**)

10. *Sophie's World*, by Jostein Gaarder, is a novel, but it is also a history of Western philosophy. (**Fused sentences**)

11. correct (**Restrictive and nonrestrictive clauses**)

12. The pre-Socratic Greek philosophers, among whom are Thales and Heraclitus, begin Sophie's lessons. (**Restrictive and nonrestrictive prepositional phrases**)

13. *Siddhartha* was written by a Westerner, yet its philosophy is Eastern. (**Fused sentences**)

14. An unabridged dictionary, which is usually expensive, can be a good investment. (**Restrictive and nonrestrictive clauses**)

15. But the *Oxford English Dictionary*, a multivolume classic, is impractical for home use. (**Appositives**)

16. correct (**Restrictive and nonrestrictive clauses**)

17. Encyclopedias that once took up much shelf space now appear on a single CD-ROM disk. (**Restrictive and nonrestrictive clauses**)

18. A thesaurus, in spite of its usefulness, can create problems. (**Restrictive and nonrestrictive prepositional phrases**)

19. Writers may choose a word with incorrect connotations, or they may select words that do not fit their context. (**Fused sentences**)

20. Beware of the thesaurus! It can be a dangerous beast. (**Comma splice**)

21-30.

"The Lottery," by Shirley Jackson, is a horror story that begins in sunshine and ends in violence. And it is more than that. The people of the town maintain an old tradition, clinging to a ritual whose meaning and purpose are not understood. This lack of understanding makes the lottery senseless, cruel, and barbaric.

Because the little boy participates in stoning his mother to death, readers are appalled. Yet they have different interpretations of the story's meaning. (**Sentence fragments**)

31. Anti-discrimination laws have given equal opportunity to job seekers. (**Subject-verb agreement**)

32. Each of the new nations will have its own constitution. (**Indefinite pronouns**)

33. Those suggestions sound like nonsense to me. (**Subject-verb agreement**)

34. correct (**Indefinite pronouns**)

35. correct (**Subject-verb agreement**)

36. Although wool carpeting is expensive, it wears well. *Carpeting* is the antecedent of the pronoun. (**Pronoun-antecedent agreement**)

37. It is difficult to follow instructions when they aren't written clearly. *Instructions* is the antecedent of the pronoun. (**Pronoun-antecedent agreement**)

38. Everyone has his or her own opinion about how to solve the problem. (**Indefinite pronouns**)

39. There are the keys that Kent misplaced. *Keys* is the subject of the verb. (**Subject-verb agreement**)

40. correct (**Subject-verb agreement**)

41. Some tortoises are long-lived; they may live for one hundred years. (**Pronoun-antecedent agreement**)

42. When someone suddenly hears a loud noise, he or she may jump. (**Indefinite pronouns**)

43. The O'Haras and the Parks share a cabin every summer. The compound subject *O'Haras and Parks* requires a plural verb. (**Subject-verb agreement**)

44. To prevent injury, the protection football players use includes shoulder pads, knee pads, mouthpieces, and helmets. *Protection* is the subject of *includes*. (**Subject-verb agreement**)

45. correct: *team* taken as a collective noun. (**Subject-verb agreement**)

46. correct. (**Subject-verb agreement**)

47. Neither Min's cat nor his dog sleeps outdoors. With *neither/nor*, if both subjects are singular, the verb is singular. (**Subject-verb agreement**)

48. In a stunning upset, the number-one team had its tail kicked. *Team* is seen as a collective noun (**Pronoun-antecedent agreement**)

49. Both Emily and Valerie enjoy Bizet's opera *Carmen*. Compound subject *Emily and Valerie* takes a plural verb. (**Subject-verb agreement**)

50. The motive for Jim's actions surprises Trisha. *Motive* is the subject of the verb. (**Subject-verb agreement**)

51. When the curling iron is heated enough, Rayna begins curling my hair. (**Dangling participles**)

52. correct (**Dangling participles**)

53. A huge boulder fell with a crash as we rounded the curve. (**Misplaced prepositional phrases**)

54. Hank finds salted or plain peanuts delicious. (**Placement of adjectives and adverbs**)

55. After we watched T.V. all evening, the dirty dishes were still on the table. (**Dangling participles**)

56. correct (**Placement of adjectives and adverbs**)

57. I read in the newspaper that the murderer had been caught. correct (**Dangling participles**)

58. Valerie saw the squirrels in the trees in the park hopping from branch to branch. (**Misplaced prepositional phrases**)

59. Because Carol was uninterested in boys, her adolescence was tranquil. (**Dangling participles**)

60. While I was waiting in line to pay, the checker bagged my groceries. (**Dangling participles**)

61. Anne, worried by financial problems, needed a job. (**Misplaced participles**)

62. correct (**Dangling participles**)

63. Since I carried a heavy suitcase, the walk from the ticket counter to the terminal seemed very long. (**Dangling participles**)

64. The problem that Karen examined confused her thoroughly. *or* The problem that Karen examined thoroughly was confusing. (**Placement of prepositional phrases**)

65. correct (**Placement of prepositional phrases**)

66. Excited about the championship, the team held a celebration in the locker room. (**Dangling participles**)

67. When it is flashing, do not pass a yellow traffic signal. (**Dangling participles**)

68. Shortly after we were seated, the waiter approached our table. (**Dangling participles**)

69. correct (**Placement of prepositional phrases**)

70. The newspaper that Myra glanced at explained the complicated situation quickly. (**Placement of adjectives and adverbs**)

71. correct (**Parallel forms with coordinating conjunctions**)

72. Hoping for a better life and anticipating California will be paradise, they set out on their journey. (**Parallelism of verbals**)

73. correct (**Parallel forms with coordinating conjunctions**).

74. Underpowered, overloaded, and leaking, the engines break down. (**Parallel forms with coordinating conjunctions**)

75. Their temporary settlements, where the migrants lived in tents or cardboard shacks, slept on the ground, and cooked over open fires, were called Hoovervilles. (**Parallelism of verbals**)

76. correct (**Parallel forms with coordinating conjunctions**)

77. After he accidentally kills a man, Tom Joad can hide run from the law or hide with his family. (**Parallel forms with coordinating conjunctions**)

78. The migrants find pleasure and amusement in telling stories and jokes, playing the harmonica, guitar, or fiddle, and dancing. (**Parallelism of verbals**)

79. When the migrants arrive in California, they are cheated, despised, and harassed. (**Parallel forms with coordinating conjunctions**)

80. correct (**Parallel forms with coordinating conjunctions**)

81. In a song popular during World War II, Americans sang about praising the Lord and passing the ammunition. (**Parallelism of verbals**)

82. The worker in "Old Man River" is tired of living and scared of dying. (**Parallel forms with coordinating conjunctions**)

83. correct (**Parallelism of verbals**)

84. correct (**Parallel forms with coordinating conjunctions**)

85. The strings of a violin can be bowed, plucked, or strummed. (**Parallel forms with coordinating conjunctions**)

86. Hot, cool and blue: the moods of jazz vary: (**Parallel forms with coordinating conjunctions**)

87. Background music in films is used to create suspense, to set a mood, and to illuminate characters. (**Parallelism of verbals**)

88. correct (**Parallelism of verbals**)

89. Michael Jackson's "moonwalk" displays gliding, stooping, and reversing direction. (**Parallelism of verbals**)

90. Emily, when exercising, enjoys calisthenics but not jogging. (**Parallelism of verbals**)

91-100.

Some students do not realize how much time it takes to write a research paper. It (pronoun shift) requires several preliminary steps. They choose a subject and restrict (tense shift) its focus. Then they (pronoun shift) need to find relevant materials in the library. Both books and periodicals are (tense shift) used in many research papers. Next they take notes. (correct) Then one (pronoun shift) must organize the notes. At this point, an outline of the paper is helpful. (correct) At last it is (tense shift) time to draft the paper, but they (pronoun shift) must also leave enough time to revise and edit it. Finally, they must compile a list of works cited. (correct) Then they must type it (tense shift) before the due date. (**Shifts**)

Grade Yourself

Circle the numbers of the questions you missed, then fill in the total incorrect for each topic. If you answered more than three questions incorrectly, you need to focus on that topic. (If a topic has less than three questions and you had at least one wrong, we suggest you study that topic also. Read your textbook, a review book, or ask your teacher for help.)

Subject: Pronouns

Topic	Question Numbers	Number Incorrect
Restrictive and nonrestrictive clauses	1, 2	
Fused sentences	3, 10, 13, 19	
Compound sentences	4, 6	
Appositives	5, 19, 15	
Restrictive and nonrestrictive prepositional phrases	7, 8, 11, 12, 13, 16, 17, 18	
Comma splice	20	
Sentence fragments	21, 22, 23, 24, 25, 26, 27, 28, 29, 30	
Subject-verb agreement	31, 33, 35, 39, 40, 43, 45, 46, 47, 49, 50	
Indefinite pronouns	32, 34, 38, 42	
Pronoun-antecedent agreement	36, 37, 41, 48	
Dangling participles	51, 52, 55, 57, 59, 60, 62, 63, 66, 67, 68	
Misplaced prepositional phrases	53, 58	
Placement of adjectives and adverbs	54, 56, 64	
Misplaced participles	61	
Placement of prepositional phrases	65, 59, 70	
Parallel forms with coordinating conjunctions	71, 73, 74, 76, 77, 79, 80, 82, 84, 85, 86, 87	
Parallelism of verbals	72, 75, 78, 81, 83, 88, 89, 90	
Shifts	91, 92, 93, 94, 95, 96, 97, 98, 99, 100	